The Peaceable Classroom

The Peaceable Classroom

Mary Rose O'Reilley, Ph.D.

English Department
University of St. Thomas
St. Paul, MN

Boynton/Cook Publishers
HEINEMANN
Portsmouth, NH

Boynton/Cook Publishers
A subsidiary of Reed Elsevier, Inc.
361 Hanover Street
Portsmouth, NH 03801-3912

Offices and agents throughout the world

The author and publisher wish to thank those who granted permission to reprint previously published material:
"The Centered Classroom" by Mary Rose O'Reilley. From *Weavings: A Journal of the Christian Spiritual Life* IV(5):21–31, 1989. Reprinted by permission of the author and The Upper Room, Nashville, TN.
"The Peaceable Classroom" by Mary Rose O'Reilley first appeared in slightly different form in *College English* (February 1984). Copyright © 1984 by the National Council of Teachers of English. Reprinted with permission.
"Silence and Slow Time: Pedagogies from Inner Space" by Mary Rose O'Reilley first appeared in *Pre/Text* II(1-2):133–43, 1990. Reprinted by permission of the author and *Pre/Text*. Arlington, TX: University of Texas.

Additional credits appear on page 160.

Library of Congress Cataloging-in-Publication Data

O'Reilley, Mary Rose.
The peaceable classroom / Mary Rose O'Reilley.
p. cm.
Includes bibliographical references.
ISBN 0-86709-328-5
1. English philology—Study and teaching—United States.
2. Classroom management—United States. 3. Teaching—Psychological aspects. 4. English teachers—United States. I. Title.
PE68.U5074 1993
428' 007'073—dc20 93-17781

Editor: Dawn Boyer
Production: Renée LeVerrier
Cover design by George McLean
Cover illustration by Anthony Chan, from *Hmong Textile Designs*, copyright © 1990 by Anthony Chan, reprinted by permission of Stemmer House Publishers, Inc.

Printed in the United States of America on acid-free recycled ♻ paper
99 98 97 96 EB 2 3 4 5

Dedicated, with love, to my children
Jude Michael Dylan O'Reilley
and
Julian Margaret O'Reilley

"Our goal is to create a beloved community and this will require a qualitative change in our souls as well as a quantitative change in our lives."

—Martin Luther King, Jr.

Contents

Foreword *ix*
Acknowledgments *xv*
Preface *xvii*

Prologue: *I Am Not Yet Born* *1*

One: *Old Lies* *19*

Two: *Inner Peace Studies and the World of the Writing Teacher* *36*

Three: *"Exterminate . . . the Brutes" and Other Notes Toward a Spirituality of Teaching* *64*

Four: *The Force that Through the Green Fuse Drives the Flower* *77*

Five: *Silence and Slow Time* *99*

Six: *The Dancing Is Difficult* *111*

Seven: *The Retro War* *120*

Eight: *The Sibyl in the Bottle* *125*

Epilogue: *The Booty of the Dove* *140*

One or Two Things *152*
Works Cited *154*
Credits *160*

Foreword

I remember the excitement I felt in 1984 when I first encountered Mary Rose O'Reilley's essay, "The Peaceable Classroom" (*College English* 46.2). Here was something new and brave—a voice saying things I was hungry to hear about issues of violence and nonviolence in teaching—central issues that are almost always ignored in our professional writing. Then in 1989 came her "Exterminate the Brutes" (*College English* 51.2), like a kick in the stomach, her second report from the war zone of her attempt to practice radical nonviolence in teaching: discouragement and indeed despair at the feelings of failure. "How could she say and publish these horrible thoughts and feelings," I thought to myself—horrible thoughts and feelings that we all have but so often run away from? It was an excruciatingly honest account of the anger one feels toward students and one's own efforts. And then she left us there.

And now this book—in which enormous idealism and optimism and equally enormous pessimism and anger have had a chance to cook together to produce something I find rich, deep, and powerful.

Gandhi said in his autobiography that everything he did in his life derived from nothing but an attempt to *tell the truth* in all matters, especially the smallest (and O'Reilley's work surely grows out of her insistence on truth telling as the cornerstone of writing). So this book constructs a wide-ranging exploration of teaching derived from her focus on *peaceableness* or *nonviolence*.

> "Those of us who persisted in a radical critique of the educational system had to invent a body of technique to replace the

old. What were we to invent it out of? I'm inventing mine out of poetry and the principles of nonviolence."[116]

She starts from the question she asked herself in graduate school, "Is it possible to teach English in such a way that people stop killing each other?" She takes a kind of pleasure in the radical nuttiness of such a question, yet it leads her to notice what people refer to as all the "little acts of violence" that go on in teaching and schooling—but she refuses to call them *little.*

It's interesting to me that so many people are trying these days to explore the possibilities of nonadversarial argument.* Something is going on now in our culture that is leading lots of us to hunger for the possibility. O'Reilley is helpful in this particular area of nonviolence, too. She shows us by example that it's possible to assert one's own point of view powerfully—genuinely to struggle and push for it ("there is a danger of merely affirming the passive, the icon of woundedness" [195])—and yet avoid the speech act of most academic arguments namely trying to demonstrate that the other person is wrong, bad, to make him feel stupid. O'Reilley helps us see the path that so many of us are trying to find: instead of trying to show the other person wrong, provide a vision to enter into, a door to walk through, a place from which to see and feel things differently ("I suggest that we look at compassion as a mode of critical inquiry"[124]).

Incidentally, one of the best ways to get people to try walking through a door or trying on a vision is by making them

---

**See* "Against Literary Darwinism: Women's Voices and Critical Discourse" by Olivia Frey, *College English* 52.5, September 1990. "Equity and Peace in the New Writing Class" by Olivia Frey, *Teaching Writing: Pedagogy, Gender, and Equity*, edited by Cynthia L. Caywood and Gillian R. Overing, SUNY Press, 1987. "Beyond Argument in Feminist Composition" by Catherine E. Lamb, *College Composition and Communication* 42 CCC42.1, February 1991. "Empathy: The Heart of Collaborative Communication" by Nathaniel Teich, *Rogerian Perspectives: Collaborative Rhetoric for Oral and Written Communication*, edited by Teich, Ablex Publishing, 1991. And, "Uses of Binary Thinking" by Peter Elbow, *Journal of Advanced Composition* 13.1, Winter 1993. "Fighting Words: Unlearning to Write the Critical Essay" by Jane Tompkins, *The Georgia Review* 42, Fall 1988.

laugh. At the moment I cannot think of a funnier book in all the field of composition. I think of Paul Diederich's classic *Measuring Growth in English* [NCTE, 1974] as another remarkably funny book. Can it be that we are in a field so mixed in earnestness that its two funniest subfields are spirituality and evaluation? ("What happens if you let all your vulnerability show? I don't know; if you have had experience along these lines, write me a letter from whatever hospital you are in"[166].)

"What if we were to take seriously the possibility that our students have a rich and authoritative inner life, and tried to nourish it rather than negate it?" [152] It's stunning to me how this sentence seems surprising and new. What else do we do in all our teaching but try to nourish our students' inner lives? English has always been a subject where we pursue what is internal—where we work on mind, intellect, imagination, feelings, internal representation—more than on mere logic, reasoning, problem-solving, communication skills. I talk about freewriting, private writing, keeping a journal, the ability to have dialogue with oneself. Yet when O'Reilley talks about the inner life as she does in this book, she makes me realize that I and most of the profession have been forgetting something central. If I remembered it more; if I asked myself, "What does today's teaching plan have to do with my students' inner life? and with *my* inner life?" Then I think I would teach differently: better, less frantic, less troubled, less chronically torn, with more calm assurance.

I'm grateful to this book for giving me courage and hope. I think it will do the same for others. I wonder if these are not the two virtues we need most now. Yes, of course we need charity and intelligence; we often fail to do something we ought to do because we're too selfish or lazy, or we do something dumb because we couldn't see what it would lead to. Yet I'm struck with how often my thoughtlessness and blindness stem from a lack of courage or hope. When I am braver and more hopeful, I am more likely to do any number of small but fruitful things: to take on an issue which normally feels too much like a hopeless morass; to notice something that needs doing and have some faith that I can be of some use; to risk getting someone mad at me; to venture in my writing or teaching into an area of perplexity or anxiety that I'd like to pursue but feel it is not legitimate or safe; to bring out into the open a subject that is just peeking out from a corner in a personal conversation or class discussion; to ask that question that normally doesn't even enter my mind; to do something about it when something unfair is said or done in my classroom or department. It seems hopeless to yearn for *charity* or *serenity* or *respect* for others in ourselves or in our students. But it seems profoundly hopeful to realize that these qualities often spring up naturally where there is courage.

Mary Rose O'Reilley doesn't talk much about courage, but her book invites courage because of how it grows so palpably out of courage: in pursuing her vision and in facing her bafflement about where this takes her. It makes me feel braver about teaching; makes me more eager to "re-enter the fray." And though she might *laugh* at me because "fray" was my instinctive metaphor for the teaching that *The Peaceable Classroom* makes me want to engage in, her laughter would be charitable. Indeed, she would be able to identify with me. Her humor in pointing out her own screwups is a central source of energy and insight in the book. Reading along, I fall into the stance of the child who says, "Tell us another story about a time when you did it wrong."

Hope. Her book is about remaining faithful to a vision. This is what I find most moving and helpful. My teaching grows out of my own hungers and visions of how things could be: a persistent sense of how things *could* be special, amazing, different; how much we could be with each other, or with language, knowledge, writing. Real learning; "the real thing" (Surely it's a deep human hunger if *CocaCola* and Henry James agree on it.) But teaching persistently fails to work as one imagines it might. (That's why I love writing: in writing we can go straight for how things ought to be.)

O'Reilley gives me hope: not by telling me how to do it, not by reassuring me that my vision is correct or that some day I'll finally get things right. Indeed it is central to her vision that we attend better to how things persist in not working and how this situation will not go away.

> "If we are being honest and attentive, I think there is always a place of discomfort in our teaching practice, a place of incongruity between our beliefs and our conduct. For many years I ignored that raw spot in myself—in fact I am good at ignoring it"[170].

There is anything but easy optimism here. ("I look forward to an eruption of spirit, but in the short term, I expect merely eruptions" [201].)

But she gives courage about *having* the vision and letting teaching grow out of it: hope that it's all right to keep putting up with things not working; that this is right, that this is a kind of holiness. The answer is not to give up the vision but to be better at living with it and playing with it, and respecting the inner struggle and disappointment as part of the real life of a teacher.

> "But I stay in teaching because all the models we have for spiritual process—religious, mythic, what have you—tell us that it doesn't matter whether we are right or wrong or successful, but merely that we remain faithful to a vision. And that when it's easy, it isn't worth much. So let me repeat and rephrase: because teaching is some kind of spiritual inquiry, what we learn is more important than what *they* learn" [110–11].

I can't wait till this book gets printed and bound. For it is a book I want to *give* to people—to buy copies and put them physically in friends' hands, send them in the mail. An odd reaction. What does it mean? If the book just had helpful ideas and a wise argument, I could simply recommend it. But there is some other quality here. I feel the book as something not merely to read but to *have*—in some sense, keep with one. It reminds me of how language can be talismanic. (It is a deep impulse to write down and tell other people quotations from things that matter to us and I have that impulse here.) A book can convey presence. (I think of an anecdote about William James: how he sent one of his books to a friend with a letter that said, in effect, "Please don't feel you have to read my book. It simply gives me deep satisfaction to imagine my book sitting on your shelf.") It's a cornerstone of speech act theory that all language is acting or doing. What I find important to note is how some words do more than others—and it seems to me that O'Reilley's words do more than most words from the profession that I've read in a long time.

Peter Elbow

Acknowledgments

These chapters are grounded in family, friendship, and collegial life. Everyone helped, but especially Margaret Hope Bacon, Peter Bien, Kenneth Boulding, Brian Nerney, Lon Otto, and Parker Palmer, who responded to early drafts. Elizabeth Bachrach Tan, Erika Scheurer, and Sherri L. Vanden Akker kindly shared the perspective of young teachers and recent graduate students. To Peter Elbow, in particular, who noticed, helped, championed, and, above all, kept doing his own work—which makes this humbler one possible—I owe the deepest debt of gratitude. I'd also like to thank Jim Vopat, without whose companionship at the Carroll College pinball machine I would never have been able to keep teaching; Peter Crysdale, who keeps reminding me of what my real job is; Michael Jordan, chair of the English department at the University of St. Thomas, who helped with reassigned time and gentle encouragement; and Joan Piorkowski, unfailing friend. Robert K. Miller's kindness fed my spirit while our working dinners fed my body. His astute marginal comments in the last critical months immeasurably sharpened the focus, as did those of Michael Mikolajczak, so perceptive of nuance. Special thanks to Carol Bly for kindly godmothering, and to R. Bruce Cutler, who read the final manuscript with a keen eye and a poet's heart. Dawn Boyer, at Heinemann, would have gotten me to write a better book if only I'd had the brains. And finally, with love and reverence, I celebrate the memory of my cherished friend and mentor, the late Professor Mulford Sibley.

The Faculty Development program of the University of St. Thomas was generous in its support during critical phases of the writing; so was the Quaker community at Pendle Hill, who provided the Helen Hole Scholarship for sabbatical support. Thank you all.

Preface

Several years ago, I wrote an article for *College English* called "The Peaceable Classroom," which argued that teaching English is an intrinsically radical act. It talked about the teacher's role in changing the structure of consciousness, and hence, the way we do intellectual and emotional business in the Western world. "The Peaceable Classroom" attempted to validate in the academy a place for consensus, cooperation, interiority, and intuition. A lot of teachers—and other people from all walks of life—wrote to say that the article had given them hope and energy, which gave *me* hope and energy to write some more. This book is the result.

I have made it out of my daily life as a teacher; indeed, I think writing can be rather like making a meal out of things you have in the kitchen. You don't have to go out for exotic ingredients. I've structured it chronologically and autobiographically so that you can enter into my life—should you choose to sit in this kitchen—and see why I think the things I do. Virginia Woolf calls this "developing in your presence a train of thought," as opposed to defending a rhetorical position.

The book, then, is not a how-to manual, still less an argument developed from premise to conclusion. It's a collection of stories, tropes, and images that nudge up against each other and try to reproduce the "analysis" as an experience, an experience I hope the reader will share the living-of. Instead of constructing an argument in theoretical terms, I am trying to "make it happen," to give you a sort of laboratory insight into the issues and problems.

Consider, merely as an example, the critical problems associated with the autobiographical stance I have chosen to develop here. One could, in a scholarly way, talk about *ethos* or *persona*, how the writer is always telling a *version* rather than a *truth*, how it's tempting to construct a puppet of the self and show it off in the best light. Instead of surveying these critical ideas, I've tried—in the prologue, for example—to expose the smoke and mirrors of the autobiographical method. I have constructed and then revised (undercut, perhaps) an authorial voice. I have tried to throw you off balance, not out of meanness, but because I am myself off balance: discovering myself as I write, getting rid of the false or limited, and trying, if not for the true, for the truer.

In writing this book, you see, I have had to ask myself how I might invite the reader into the fullest possible participation, because the book is about making connections. One of my college philosophy professors, Dr. James Ian Campbell, used to be exceptionally good at this. He did not lecture about philosophical questions in some dead and detached way. Actor, magus, and trickster all at once, he would summon up the problem in its dangerous contrariety and let its energy fill the classroom. We would sit tensely with Descartes, tucked up by his famous stove, involved to our fingertips in the *cogito*. We couldn't leave class until we had been assured that something existed outside the self. We had forgotten, indeed, that we were *in* class. I wish that I could write as well as Jamie Campbell taught, but I have set myself the goal, at least, of leading you to feel my subject in bone as well as brain.

Poems, of course, work this way at the cellular level of exchange; and perhaps it would help to say that my method of arrangement here is more poetic than discursive. As I said earlier, the book evolves by repetition and the logic of images rather than by thesis and example. It seems to me that there are bells that ring for each of us, sounding through the babble of daily life: deep tones that call us at the most profound levels of our ability to hear. I have tried to set some bells ringing in this text (it seems pretentious to say so, though they are not *my* bells but imports): an idea in chapter two that resonates in chapter six, a phrase here that calls to a phrase later. I have organized the book in this poetic or symphonic way; therefore you will not get a full discussion of something all at once: you will hear a bell note, and when next you hear it, you will, I hope, bring forward not only a memory of its last sounding but also what you have made of it, you yourself, in the levels and layers of your own consciousness. That is the method I have devised—however inadequately it may be realized—for letting the reader engage with me in the writing of this book. A better craftsman would do a better job, but that is at least the job I have tried to do. Only in the reader's consciousness will the story be whole, and every reader will read a slightly different story.

Take away from it what forms in your own mind. I have been conscientious in withholding details: come into my kitchen, but don't expect recipes. I've tried to convey a number of concerns about peacemaking, right livelihood, compassion, social justice, and contemplation, but I cannot teach you how to "use" these spiritual principles. I can only stammer out the images of my world and invite you to sit with them. If you take in whatever is valuable to you, you will make different choices from the ones I have made, but I'm sure, wise ones. Then you can tell me about *your* world. That's the spirit in which these essays are written.

Mary Rose O'Reilley

The Peaceable Classroom

Prologue

I Am Not Yet Born

I am not yet born; O fill me
With strength against those who would freeze my
humanity, would dragoon me into a lethal automaton
would make me a cog in a machine, a thing with
one face, a thing, and against all those
who would dissipate my entirety, would
blow me like thistledown hither and
thither or hither and thither
like water held in the
hands would spill me.

Let them not make me a stone and let them not spill me,
Otherwise kill me.

—Louis MacNeice, "Prayer Before Birth" (215)

The summer after I graduated from college in 1967, I had a job teaching "emotionally disturbed" children at a private school. SLBP the program was called—a noise like greasy bubbles down the drain: Special Learning/Behavior Problems. I worked with second-through-fourth graders, tutoring them individually under the direction of a head teacher. We had a full complement of psychologists, dieticians, behavior modifiers, physical therapists, etc., on board, but we never had enough teachers or aides.

The therapists seemed to have a nice time of it; I would go by the glass doors of their offices on the way to my classroom and see the soles of big brown shoes up on the desks. Around the coffee machine they argued about whether behavior problems were rooted in the fore brain or the hind brain, in the acytylcholine or the toilet training; in their spare time, they psychoanalyzed the teachers. That summer they taught me that all poets (I was a poet then) are minimally brain damaged (MBD), a curious hypothesis that still has the ability to stir my powers of speculation.

On my way to SLBP, I would look enviously into the orderly classrooms of the merely retarded who seemed to swim along like astronauts in slow and silent space. By contrast, frenetic motion characterized my students: thirty-two kids, revolving, undulating, and screeching among the desks as the Head Teacher tried to keep order. She screamed a lot, and I patrolled around the periphery, watching for murder and pyromania in the ranks. (Many of our students were fire starters, a metaphor with multiple applications in the teaching business.) Some of them were also—I do not know how to put this delicately—what we called "mad shitters" (MS). Teachers could never leave a book or sweater unattended, lest they find it marked with some student's personal tribute.

One of my jobs was to take children out for individual tutoring, bandaging, suturing, pants changing, whatever it was they needed. When things got completely out of hand, we sent a few scapegoats to the principal.

It was whispered in the halls that the principal, who wore cowboy boots and played country-western music over the intercom, "knocked the kids around a little." But we sent the children to him when we ran out of options, feeling something like switch handlers in the Nazi railyards. They came back red-faced and blubbering, but they would quiet down for awhile.

The world of school, I was discovering, is as morally ambiguous as any back alley. Certainly I did not, at the time, question the principal's disciplinary measures. We were all too busy trying to survive and minimize the damage the kids could do to each other. Besides, who among us had not been slapped or brutalized both at home and at school? That went with growing up in lower-middle-class culture (and other cultures as well, as I now know). We were even quite capable of associating physical punishment with love; indeed, I took for granted that the principal cared deeply about the well-being of the children and the school. He was good at his job on these terms: he spoke plainly, treated everyone fairly, defended the weak, punished aggressors, and kept the school from burning down. He embodied, that is, all of the virtues of the American frontier hero. It was OK, by our perverse code, for such a man in such a school to hit children; some might have called it his duty, though he was not supposed to do it often, or to enjoy it. The working archetype was, I think, Gary Cooper in *High Noon*.

I suppose somebody was making money off that school, and the parents were happy to have their children's hind brains under observation some place far from home. At best we managed custodial care and, in retrospect, I realize that no one expected any better of us.

The weakest of the children—who tended to be the most sane—were doomed to inattention at the very least. One quite normal little boy, for example, had been levered into our prestigious program by wealthy parents who preferred to label their son "disturbed" rather than merely "slow." (Some labels have more social cachet than others.) He would sit quietly in the midst of chaos with his hand raised. He was a good parochial school boy. He may be sitting there yet.

A good parochial school girl myself, it shamed me that, for no reason, I hated some of the kids. (With "reason" one could have hated all of them.) A month before I had been sitting in an air-conditioned classroom reading moral theology. Where had I taken a wrong turn and slipped, like Alice, through the glass door of this primal world? For starters, I hated Genna and her brother, Greg, with their yellow hair, sallow skin, and slack jaws. They were well-behaved, quiet, and stupid. They needed a lot of tutoring because they had never mastered the simplest fact. Knowing what I know now, I suspect they had been starved and abused from birth; they looked inbred and frail, with Gothic hollows where the eyes should go. Moral theology had failed to teach me how to love them; my senior exam had required me merely to know how to proceed if a priest went mad and consecrated a bread truck.

I didn't "take out" Genna and Greg if I could avoid it; plenty of psychologists, in any case, vied for this tractable pair.

I wasn't fond of Frankie either. He was brilliant and wound very tight. He was the only child I worked with that summer who actually produced something: a report on whales, which he tried to make the other children listen to, vibrating, when he failed, like a first-year teacher.

Danny, by contrast, I loved. He was the worst kid in the school, probably one of the worst kids in the world—biter, kicker, fuck-you screamer, and Olympian firestarter. He was overweight and clumsy with a pudgy, pushed-in face. He looked like the fat kid in the Our Gang comedies, though comedy was not his line. I took him out whenever I could.

No matter how much he bit, kicked, and torched things, I couldn't stop smiling at Danny. Love is illogical. His badness was so perfect, so whole, it seemed to verge on holiness. On the last day of school, Danny leaped on me and dug in his nails—nothing new—but "Don't leave," he said.

As for that, I had some place to go.

Many of the teachers got drunk at the end of the day. We would sort out our ruined books and sweaters, go out together, and drink in the bar across the street from school. We must have been full of feeling to need to drink so much, but we never let on. Indeed, I remember most of my colleagues as automatons, perfectly groomed and dressed, never flustered. They didn't care for the principal, not because of the rumors about corporal punishment, but because he defiantly wore the wrong kind of clothes (fashion, that summer, dictated lime and yellow polyester) and because he liked what was then considered working-class music. Teaching represented for many of us in those days a separation from blue collar origins, and we were always afraid our vowels would slip or some drawling and booted rebel would call into question our middle-brow assumptions.

For my part, I had dropped out of college a couple of times and, in my frenzy to catch up, had become a relentless Jude-the-Obscure-like studier. I would read Frederick Copleston's histories of philosophy on the bus along with daily selections from Sertillanges' *The Intellectual Life.* (I had reached one of Sertillanges' most lyrical passages—on the duties of an intellectual's wife—when somebody stole the book.) In the evening, faithful to my hard-won B.A., I rushed off to avant-garde theater and watched plays about the impossibility of communication. I saw "The Bald Soprano," "Krapp's Last Tape," and that play where people talk to each other from garbage cans.

I tried to separate some supposed real self from the daily detour of teaching, but the plays merely carried me back to the classroom, an antimatter world I had fallen into while looking for a summer job. For sixteen years I had gone to school, and now I was going to *anti*school, black hole school, in the twilight zone.

At ten-thirty every day the bell would ring and the teachers would begin to slink out for "break." There were never enough teachers to cover, so, crazy as it sounds, we often left the kids alone. As soon as the teachers went away, the students started to behave. Through the glass door, we would see them take their crayons and go silently to work.

We could never figure it out.

The Pedagogy of the Depressed

It's surprising that the experiences that leave the deepest imprint on our lives are often of short duration—a week here, a summer vacation there changes everything. In a new scene, our eyes are open, our perceptions dilated. We bring our sense of self (or our character armor) to bear against the assault of newness, and details stand out in stark relief. I taught at Black Hole School for only three months: what did I know about its inner workings, really? What gave an experience I barely understood the power to alter my life? What gives me the right to make harsh judgments about it, on the one hand, and to carry away, on the other, a sense of intimate connection with people I will probably never meet again?

I left the place with a sense of psychic nausea. A lot that went on there was wrong by anyone's standards, but worse than the badness was the moral neutrality—The endless nail-polishing in the teachers' lounge, the talk about fashion interspersed with heartless gossip about the students, objectifying them with psychiatric labels and jargon. Dante would have put us teachers in the vestibule of hell, too depraved for heaven, too boring to appreciate a creative punishment. Wallowing around in this slough of ambiguity, I admired the principal, who seemed, by contrast, strong, honorable, and clear. I wish that back then someone had been able to model an alternative archetype to our cowboy leader: a hero who did not, at the end of the movie, go for his gun. But no one did.

And Black Hole School had let me see more than I cared to of my own inner darkness, of which my talent for hating students was only a sliver. At the same time I should note the emergence of a single shaft of light: a talent for loving them, loving, especially, students like Danny who were headed right off the moral map. Any good Jungian, any good Zen master (I had begun to study Japanese Buddhism that summer) could have told me that opposing forces always exist in dynamic relation to each other, but I did not know that then, and the complexity of it all made me queasy.

Looking for some kind of antidote, I fled to graduate school. I wrote out my applications in longhand to the University of Chicago and the University of Wisconsin–Milwaukee, got into both places and chose UWM. They told me that besides being able to study literature, I would get to teach a class of freshmen all my own. This appealed to me enormously. I did not know that when you become a TA you have just, in effect, been handed a paint brush by Tom Sawyer. Nor, when I found out, did I mind, for I needed the challenge of painting that particular fence.

To my good fortune, UWM was not a chic place. I suspect that the real business of the university in those days was surviving (shades of Black Hole School) the daily floods of undergraduate students, who were products of a more-or-less open admissions policy. This focus kept the graduate program from working up any pretensions. The faculty ran to strong scholars who talked about texts they seemed to like—a fair and plain model of graduate education—and for years I didn't know there was any other way of conceiving a program. We grad students studied hard and were taught well, but the freshmen kept us too busy to develop any arty theoretical focus. Each TA was indeed solely responsible for two sections of English 101, and that was not a bad thing. It meant that in our first year of graduate study, we had already begun to poise ourselves in the central balancing act of teaching English: on the one hand, respect for a complex tradition (which you are anxious to *profess*) and, on the other, the need to support a timorous learner (whose *teacher* you are). In this framework, subject to such real constraints and exigencies, we took in the required information about Jacobean Drama. If someone had tried to engage us on questions of social-epistemic discourse, we simply wouldn't have had time. Fortunately no one did. Instead we hung around debating questions like: Is there an idea you'd give your life for?

I had left my summer job at Black Hole School with a number of questions about *right livelihood* (to use the Buddhist formulation): does your vocation embody an ideal of compassion, or does it not? At twenty-two I knew, though I could perhaps not have put it into words, that second only to what happens between parent and child, what happens in the classroom determines the shape of culture and evolution of consciousness. Despite the disappointments of Black Hole School, I wanted to be a teacher.

I was young when I began teaching college. Some of my students were Vietnam veterans, some were draft resisters, many were draft dodgers. The veterans didn't want to do my stupid theme assignments ("The New Morality on Campus"), or if they did, they wanted to do it in what Ken Macrorie—that maverick genius comp teacher—would later call "authentic voice." One of the first student essays I took home, cast in the epistolary mode, began "Dear Alice, I'm sorry I knocked you up." Parochial education had not prepared me for this sentence. I didn't even know what it meant. "Knocked up?" I asked my more worldly colleagues. They looked at me with pity.

There was a student named Zach who came from a German-speaking farm family. He had two major interests: football, which he loved, and the draft, which he was scheming to avoid by maintaining his student deferment. His essays usually had a sort of formulaic beginning: "HUT was the cry!" Since I hadn't learned how to teach yet, I failed him in EN 101. He wrote me a note that read, "Dear Miss, please tell me why I flunk English." We had a conference. It wasn't that I didn't appreciate his hut-mantra, I told him in so many words, it was that he hadn't mastered the rudiments of English grammar and syntax. He told me, angrily, that I was writing him a ticket to Vietnam, turning him into cannon fodder. On the subject of the grade I was implacable—to change one's mind was a sign of *weakness,* I then believed—but the conference gnawed at my conscience for years. (Those who like to hear how stories turn out may be reassured to know that Zach managed to fail the draft physical as well as English, and after working his way up from coach, he became a grade school principal.)

What complicated the situation for those of us who were graduate teaching assistants in the sixties—what skewed our perception of the moral world of college teaching—was Vietnam. We didn't know how to teach very well, and many quasi-open admissions students didn't know how to learn very well. Yet there we young teachers were, evaluating essays and giving our first hesitant grades. My generation of teachers began to worry about grading because grading was a life-or-death proposition. We had to make some connections pretty quickly between our classrooms and the war outside. We began to change our methods because the methods by which we ourselves had learned did not work for open admissions students, and we did not want our students, as a consequence of our inept pedagogy, to be killed. We began to see that grading is at least metaphorically a violent act, because in 1967, it was *literally* a violent act.

"Is it possible to teach English so that people stop killing each other?" Ihab Hassan—then beginning his tenure as a distinguished professor at UWM—dropped this question into one of our colloquia for teaching assistants. We shuffled our feet. Was he kidding? Maybe we had heard wrong.

But for me the question would not go away, and nothing in the intervening years has made it go away.

An Alternate Version

I have been writing about nonviolent pedagogy for five or six years, trying to come to terms with Black Hole School and the disproportionate intensity that still attaches itself to the memory of my early teaching years. And now that I have written this much, I have to say, well, I'm not sure I have told the story with precise accuracy.

I teach a class called "The Personal Essay." Students write about their own lives and experiences; we study other writers who do that like Annie Dillard, E. B. White, Carol Bly, and George Orwell. One of the issues that always rises in a class like this is: Do I have to tell the truth about my life? A more complicated question may be, *can* I tell the truth about my life?

There was a country-western song that went, "We live in a two-story house / She has her story and I have mine." Personal writing leads us to see multiple levels in the house of truth: we deal in *versions* of reality. We settle on a story we can live with, not only because it's hard to be honest but also because our minds keep trying to create order. Order, as any freshman writer knows, requires us to craft a beginning, middle, and end, with transitional devices in place to ensure coherence. Organization, then, always violates, to some degree, the Real. Any version—any story, poem, or argument—frames reality in its own terms, and they are likely to be terms that serve our ego—or terms that save our sanity.

Merely because the critical/moral question is so complicated and so crucial, I am fairly strict with my students in expecting accuracy in the personal essay. Since it's hard to give an honest account, it's important to sketch the details as precisely as one can. Let's try for a kind of *faithfulness.* Let's try not to bluff and waffle.

That is why I pause here, forced to evaluate the accuracy of my narration. I think, for one thing, that the story has hardened into the easy formulas of the *Bildungsroman*—so eager was I, as a young woman, to go on the hero's quest.

Therefore I must try to revisit the details and see if I can call up some deeper truth.

I have painted myself as a naive young person, but I did not lack knowledge or experience; I lacked whatever quality of consciousness connects knowledge and experience to the deep, churning reaches of the mind. Much of what I "knew" was inaccessible to my daily round of thought. I have begun to write as though my interest in the phenomenology of violence rose out of some objective, scientific concern that suddenly flared into life on my first teaching job. But now I realize that the scent of blood that came to me at Black Hole School was nothing I had not smelled before. In midcareer, I have a better perspective on family life in the 1940s. I can look through the old album, not so much interested in photos of my cute little self, as with an eye for the background details of our early life on an air force base: the uniforms, the bomber squadrons, the quonset huts. I can see the larger pattern, the not-I. And I realize that most of the pattern was determined by my parents' war.

Childhood in the 1950s went on against a background of perfectly constructed surfaces. How eagerly those young men and women of my parents' generation put the war behind them, built their orderly rows of boxes across the prairie. My sister—who is working on her doctorate in family social science—could tell you how the lie was framed by popular culture: *The past does not exist. What you saw you did not see.* I think of my Navy uncle, coming back from combat to three generations of us living together in a four-room apartment. For years we thought we knew all we needed to know about him—we had seen *South Pacific*, the musical.

If I bring this primal scene into my own consciousness, I hope I bring it into the light for others of my generation so that we will better understand who we are. I go to my grade school reunions now, and I see the child-faces of my friends rise like mysterious, innocent fish behind the eyes of their midlife weariness, and I think about how we all swam through the war. My cousin—son of the uncle who survived two years of combat in the South Pacific—has spent his life as a policeman in Watts. And I have spent mine as a college teacher, trying to define a pedagogy of nonviolence. Both of us, swimming through the war.

This is not the indignant book some of my colleagues have hoped for. It is full of compromise. During the Gulf War, for example, one of my professor-friends launched a proposal to drive our ROTC contingent off campus, and I found myself unable to support it. For one thing, I want those cadets right here on a liberal arts campus where they can listen to more versions of the story. For another, the position I have taken requires the checks and balances of theirs. It seems important that many opposing communities exist in balance, polishing each other up like rocks in a river bed, with the friction of daily contact.

If I had written this book twenty years ago, it might have been angrier. Even ten years ago, I was pretty feisty: reading the *Bhagavad Gita* and badgering my teacher about what I perceived to be Arjuna's co-optation. It seemed to me then that Arjuna had it right in the beginning, stuck in compassion, refusing to fight. When he accepted the burden of his destiny and went into battle, I would maintain, he made the wrong decision. My professor would gently tell me that karma yoga did not seem to be my spiritual path, and perhaps I should get back to Zen Buddhism. But now, today, I understand Arjuna better, and see that he had, as my father and uncles had, a different weight to carry than my own. And, in the end, *he simply carried it.*

Today, I set these family meditations down beside the story of Black Hole School. It's another slant, though still not the whole truth. Ultimately, I am not interested in convincing anybody of my "position." Argument can be (though it is not necessarily) a form of intellectual violence. We pile up evidence as the kids in my neighborhood used to pile up snowballs, each with a rock in the middle, on the rims of their winter forts. If the other side has more rocks, we concede. I've been at department meetings like that; I've stockpiled my own missiles. And I'm venal enough to say that if that kind of discourse created a good result, I'd probably stick with it. But such victories create an undercurrent that pulls a community to pieces in the end.

By contrast, as Virginia Woolf wrote in *A Room of One's Own*, "I am going to do what I can to show you how I arrived at this position. . . . I am going to develop in your presence as fully and freely as I can the train of thought which led me to think this (4)." I am less interested in winning points than I am in conversion. Conversion requires that the reader come inside the position, try it out, co-create, and, in co-creating, assent to whatever captures the spirit. As Woolf continues, "One can only give one's audience the chance of drawing their own conclusions as they observe the limitations, the prejudices, the idiosyncrasies of the reader (4)." As I tell my story, I fear that I will simultaneously discover it, and no doubt that will try the patience of any reader who delights in seamless surfaces.

With that, I loop back again to the beginning of my teaching days, understanding at least one thing I did not understand when I began writing this book, much less when I began teaching college. My own war experience, if you will allow the phrase, was determining many of my "objective" thoughts and actions, and I had no idea that that was going on. I had been educated, from high school on, in the rational/Thomistic intellectual tradition. It was a sound preparation for scholarly work, but it did not sufficiently account for what was personal, subconscious, and vaguely *felt.* "Girls"— the nuns would say, for at my schools we were all girls—"what you feel is not important. What is important is what *is.* Error, girls, has no rights." The phrase "I feel . . . ," in the early corridors of my education, was anathema. We were to *think.* The value of this education so supremely outweighed its negative side—especially in the way it encouraged women to serious scholarly commitment—that I gratefully forgive its slighting of our subjective world. If it were not for the paramilitary rigor of my schooling, I would not have been standing in front of a college class at twenty-two, ready to bleat about Kierkegaard. I would never have been able to transcend that four-room apartment at the end of World War II.

But I stood there pretty ignorant of what—besides Thomas Aquinas' Sixteen Precepts for Study—was moving my mental processes. I was ignorant of the elaborate programs and pathways my neural system had built to deal with "war," "danger," and "violence." Nothing in my culture had encouraged me to take into account the personal experience that determined this mental wiring. I would argue that many of my generation shared the same wiring, and the unconsciousness.

As if in some perverted fairy tale, then, my generation of young college teachers was given a weird task to perform, weirder than gathering up a maiden's scattered pearls or bringing home some monster's singing leaves. Like all the best mythological tasks, it was one to which we were uniquely unsuited. We were supposed to decide who went to Vietnam and who did not.

Learning the Classics

I was seven months pregnant when I went to my first job interviews at the annual meeting of the Modern Language Association (MLA). In those days before the women's movement had begun to effect any real change in law or consciousness, department chairs would say things to me like, "Well, my wife thought she'd want to teach after the baby came, but she hasn't worked in fifteen years." They'd ask me whether, in the future, I intended to practice birth control. One man said, "We'll talk to Mary after she gets rid of that belly." Another put a shot of whiskey in front of me and asked if I could drink like a man.

I was so happy just to have interviews.

I bring up this history because in a little while I'll need to make some connections between feminism and pacifism, and to show how peace issues get mixed up with justice issues. Also, I have to account for a stretch of time spent outside academic life and the things that happened to clarify my sense of the relationship between people with power and people on the margins.

I wouldn't have been waddling around MLA if I hadn't, at that time, needed a job to support my family. As it turned out, I got a one-year appointment at Carroll College in Waukesha, Wisconsin. But then, family convulsions drew me to the East Coast and a string of part-time jobs. Much of this time I was living in public housing, collecting food stamps and medical assistance, walking in the long line of mothers who get up before light and ride the buses into town with sleeping children in their arms. I did not do any of this bravely, humbly, or well. Small writing jobs came my way, including one with a community organization helping household workers, mostly black, to get a minimal employee benefit plan. The last position in particular taught me a lot about institutional power politics. One vignette stands out: we had organized an informational meeting that would bring together wealthy white women and black household workers to talk about their respective situations. The workers explained how hard it was to get along without social security benefits, without health coverage, sick leave, and so on. One of the wealthy matrons took the microphone and said, "But you must understand that if I were to extend those benefits, I wouldn't be able to afford a maid." An elderly black woman made her way slowly to the podium. I had seen her the night before as we made our preparations in the church basement, all of us crying and singing and carrying on. She took the microphone and, with as much authority as I've ever seen a human being muster, she stared the matron down. "Honey," she answered, "you can't afford no maid." (This movie often runs through my mind when we try to negotiate benefits for adjunct faculty.)

Living in the projects downstairs from a man who occasionally shot holes in the ceiling, across the hall from a man who dressed up like Santa Claus and abused children, and piling up my glassware on the windowsills every night to warn me of intruders—I thought I was in moral outer space (this being merely a privileged white girl's take on short-term deprivation). But really I was just in school. I learned a lot of scams, the most useful of which was how to audit college courses for free. I took two years of classical Greek that way and seminars from several famous scholars. For all you know, your classes may be full of welfare mothers scrabbling through the *Crito*, and maybe somebody should put a stop to it.

Finally I got a responsible, though marginal, job as a lobbyist in Washington, D.C., working for a coalition of women's organizations. I spent my first year in D.C. stymied by the corruption, but my second—as I learned how to work the place—amazed at the integrity and intelligence of the support staff, the people back in the offices who pull the strings of the political puppets. And I met some senators and congressmen—the ones who never seem to make the news—who were wise and good, and a few rich people who devote their lives to the common welfare. What a complicated world.

My next job brought me back to the Midwest and the lower levels of academic administration—I had no desire to linger there. My goal all this time had been simply to get back in the classroom. And it was not until 1978—six years after I finished my dissertation on Hilda Doolittle and the Imagists—that I pounced on the first college teaching job that came my way.

St. Thomas College, then, was a small, conservative Catholic liberal arts college. (It is now a university with an enrollment close to ten thousand.) For most of its history, it had been a men's college, going coed only a year before I arrived. It's a wonder they hired me, an avowed pacifist with a résumé full of radical organizations.

Indeed, they hired me with a number of caveats. I was to keep a low profile. I was not to wear denim, with its radical associations. I was not to say anything in public to embarrass the college. During the tense early years, the president of the college and I had at least one long, heart-to-heart conversation in which each of us told, in the most personal terms, why we had our particular feelings about denim and war. I respected him enormously after that, and this respect did more than any rule or threat could do to keep me from unleashing the more excessive ranges of my temperament.

That conversation with the president had important consequences for me. Because he told me his personal story, I could enter into his situation. It is love, after all—and such a conversation is a variety of love—that keeps the moral world with its irreconcilable oppositions from flying apart like a stunned asteroid. His honesty confounded my radical posturing. I had trained myself in all those church basements always to speak out. He was patiently giving me good reason to shut up. He listened to me, too. Maybe I told him some things about women and children he didn't (being a priest) know. I told him that I might not always be able to keep quiet, but that I'd try to give him advance warning of any seismic eruptions. It was a good bargain. (Just this morning, we met in the quad and chatted about the peace studies program. "You ought to have some material in there about domestic abuse," he told me. Everything comes full circle.)

Thus it was that at St. Thomas College in 1978, I began to explore seriously the dialectics of peace and justice, differently for sure than I would have done on the streets—more inwardly, because my outward motions were under a degree of constraint. It was kind of like writing a sonnet.

One

Old Lies

"*D*ulce et Decorum Est" makes a clear and unmistakable connection between war and classroom teaching. Wilfred Owen addressed it to a grade school teacher named Jessie Pope who had written a naively patriotic poem to boost enlistment:

> If in some smothering dream, you too could pace
> Behind the wagon that we flung him in,
> And watch the white eyes writhing in his face,
> His hanging face, like a devil's sick of sin;
> If you could hear, at every jolt, the blood
> Come gargling from the froth-corrupted lungs
> Obscene as cancer, bitter as the cud
> Of vile, incurable sores on innocent tongues—
> My friend, you could not tell with such high zest
> To children ardent for some desperate glory,
> The Old Lie: Dulce et decorum est
> Pro patria mori.
>
> —Wilfred Owen, "Dulce et Decorum Est" (55)

Are we telling the Old Lie, he wanted to know, or are we not? After my years in Washington, I could see that St. Thomas College was, as every institution is, a microcosm of society's larger struggle with the ethical issues of war and peace. We had a flourishing ROTC program and also (as the need arose) a draft resisters' support group. At one of my first commencements, Archbishop John Roach put nuclear disarmament before us as a pro-life issue, but to many this was a new and startling juxtaposition. Today we have a flourishing peace studies program, but many things had to happen before that went into place.

In this atmosphere of healthy ambivalence, I developed in the early 1980s a course called "War and the Modern Imagination." How simple and quaint its agenda looks to me now with so many of my colleagues engaged in provocative research on conflict resolution, on Vietnam literature, and on multinational and multicultural peace issues. In this chapter I will review the major premises of that course (and the things I took away from it) almost as an exercise in archeology—if only because the things I learned that semester form the basis of the analysis I am trying to pursue in this book.

In examining a range of war literature including Stephen Crane's *The Red Badge of Courage*, *The Collected Poems of Wilfred Owen*, Ernest Hemingway's *A Farewell to Arms*, T. S. Eliot's *The Waste Land*, Joseph Heller's *Catch 22*, and Kurt Vonnegut's *Slaughterhouse-Five*, I hoped merely to explore the implications of Paul Fussell's thesis (in *The Great War and Modern Memory*) that war—trench warfare in particular—is one of the central organizing metaphors of twentieth-century experience. War literature was not my "area"; I wished merely to discover with my students the ways in which we have all been marked by war, how the history or fact or imminent possibility of violent confrontation conditions and defines us as humans.

"Is it possible to teach English so that people stop killing each other?" I was still struggling with Ihab Hassan's question. And how, in practice, does one effectively struggle with such a question? If we really don't know how to do something, if we really don't understand a process, if we are, like Arjuna, stuck in compassion, refusing to accept the burden of our destiny, then it's time to throw open all the doors and windows and proceed inductively. The old myths say that when you are in a quandary you should untie your shoes, unbraid your hair, unbind the ribbons and laces so that the vital spirit can flow freely. It was in "War and the Modern Imagination" that I first applied this principle to the formulation of a syllabus.

At that point, I wanted simply to read a body of war literature and reflect with my students on what happened. I wanted them to tell me what they noticed and see what we could make of their observations. I didn't know what would happen after that.

As I prepared to teach the course and puzzled over how to present the material in the classroom, another concern forced itself on my attention. As a pacifist (but one could easily say, As a Lutheran, As a Thomist, As one concerned for the preservation of the humpbacked whale) I felt the need to make connections between my personal beliefs and what happens in the classroom, the same as I wish students to make connections between their personal worlds and the texts we study. I wondered if one could identify and follow a distinctively pacifist approach to teaching about war. Excluding propaganda. Excluding polemics.

I had wondered for some time what my Quaker friends meant when they spoke (somewhat ungrammatically) of "doing nonviolent discipline." Pacifism has for most people a connotation of "non-doing," a bias my students sometimes reflect when they spell it "passivism." I wondered what the "discipline" of it might be and how one might proceed to "do" it.

Searching for formulas and finding none, I turned to the writings of the eighteenth-century Quaker abolitionist John Woolman. Woolman's challenge is a very practical one. Recognizing that individuals (then as now) may feel very little control over the sources of power that determine our destiny and survival as a species, Woolman urges us to begin by making peace within our small spheres of influence. We ought, he says, to "look upon our treasures, the furniture of our houses, and garments, and try whether the seeds of war have nourishment in these our possessions" (241).

By extension, I wondered if we can discover the seeds of war in the interactions of the typical classroom or wherever our treasures happen to lie. The most superficial examination of this question would suggest that we convey attitudes about power in the kinds of questions we ask, in the presence or absence of discussion, in grading policies, and in classroom atmosphere. The teacher uses authority validly or invalidly. She respects or does not respect individual vision. She is the center of force.

A Call From the North

A few days ago, somebody called me from a summer cabin up North. He was lying on his dock, trailing his fingers in the water, and talking on his cellular phone. He said, "I just read one of your articles. Somebody left it up here in the lodge. And what I want to know is, can I do this kind of analysis in my own world?"

"What do you do?" I asked.

"I teach business administration."

"Well sure. I don't see why not."

"So . . . we ask ourselves whether what we're doing makes for a violent outcome, or not . . ."

"Yes."

"And then . . ."

"Well, that's what's unpredictable." Then, I thought, all hell breaks loose. When you tinker with one little part of a vast system, you soon find that all your assumptions are called into question, not only about your discipline, but about your culture and how the universe is put together in its private parts. If I had known at the beginning of that journey how trying it would prove, I would never have had the courage to begin. Certain questions if asked relentlessly can give you an interesting life.

At St. Thomas College in the early 1980s, I was simply asking to what extent it might be possible and conducive to learning to disarm oneself in the classroom—while retaining one's responsibility to raise certain important questions, to evaluate responses, and, in this flawed universe, to assign grades. As I look back on this naive question, I have to snicker. Did I not know, for example, as Jerry Farber—who wrote *The Student as Nigger*—would later respond, that grades are not part of the system, they *are* the system. And who gets to decide what questions are important? And what lies behind these cultural assumptions? And how far back do we have to go in our questioning? Do we have to poke the bones of Aristotle, of Mother Earth herself? And what inner capacity for faithfulness—as Joseph Conrad might say—could keep us on course through such an inquiry?

What perhaps distracted me from the complexity of my agenda was that my question, pedagogically, was not really a new one (John Holt and Ivan Illich, among others, had explored it most recently). I merely wanted to ask it specifically in the context of nonviolent discipline. As I tried to imagine a system of education that would prepare people to make peace rather than war—and *making* peace is different from *enjoying* it—certain priorities emerged: I wanted students to talk to each other freely, and I wanted them all to talk so that no insight might be lost; I wanted them to learn from each other as well as from me; I wanted them to experience both the energy and limitations of group effort; I wanted the atmosphere of the classroom to be amicable yet serious; and, while all this was going on, I didn't want to be taken advantage of. I started with a general intuition that the truly peaceable classroom would teach students to respect each other and the truth, to attend to that of wisdom in each contribution whether from teacher or student. To listen thus attentively, to question thus seriously, is not to undermine authority but to increase sensitivity to its authentic voice.

My first task, then, was to find out what kind of individuals I had in that classroom; my second was to help them build communities of support. Self-portraits written on the first day of class yielded the usual motley: a seminarian interested in social justice, a punk rocker, a reentry woman, a blind old gentleman in the senior citizens program, a business major trying to satisfy her communications requirement, and so on. The course attracted them for various reasons. One was a pacifist, another an amateur military historian fascinated by guns, tanks, submarines, and all the technology of war; the business major liked Hemingway; another student, a sociologist, was interested in the phenomenon of violence.

As students came into "War and the Modern Imagination," they were assigned to groups of five with whom they were required to meet weekly for discussion and sharing of essays. The first week's work on *A Farewell to Arms*, then, would begin not with a lecture from the teacher, but with consideration of a student essay. These essays were not intended as finished products, and students were encouraged to revise, combine, or discard them as the class progressed. I wanted them to feel free to make false starts verbally and on paper. They were, however, discouraged from consulting secondary sources while writing their first drafts.

I think that students (beginners in particular) write better essays about what they themselves *notice* than about what they have been told by critics and teachers to look out for. In so doing, they collectively raise most of the important questions a good critic would raise and discover new byways of thought often untravelled by earlier commentators. Bumbling along this way, the student learns to connect her personal world to the world of the text. She starts to listen to those idiosyncratic promptings all of us carry around in our genetic material so vitally important to our real education, which much of our "schooling" discourages us from listening to. The writing/discussion group, in its turn, confronts the lonely scribbler with a searching, arguing, supporting, contesting community: within this framework each one can incubate and question an individual vision.

Such essays permit the teacher to base subsequent lectures and discussion on material students have already struggled with and have questions about. Typically in my course, students talked about their essays with me or with their small groups on Monday; more discussion followed on Tuesday, Wednesday, and Friday. In preparation for Tuesday's class I could read essays and pull out important ideas for analysis and amplification. The opinions of critics could be juxtaposed with student readings; doubts, theories, and questions could be aired. One could be fairly certain at all times of how students were responding to the material.

I am writing here at some length about daily teaching practice so that people unfamiliar with any but the lecture-centered classroom can get a sense of what an alternative style might feel like. I was inching my way, at this point, into an approximation of nonviolent discipline in the classroom. Today such strategies have become standard operating procedure in many English classes, or, depending where you are in the great Möbius strip of culture, they may already have become old-fashioned—under attack from those who believe in a return to traditional classroom discipline. Perhaps it will help if I simply tell about the journey I took. It is not the only path one can take, but it is the only path that explains where I came out of the woods.

What Happened

> A being deprived of the function of unreality is neurotic as well as a being deprived of the function of the real. . . . If the function of opening out, which is precisely the function of the imagination, does not perform well, perception itself remains obtuse.
>
> — Gaston Bachelard, "L'air et les songes" in *On Poetic Imagination and Reverie* (xxvii)

I wanted my students to learn about war. I did not want to send them to war but to literature and then to bring back the news. Our goal had been to read a body of war literature and reflect on what happened. Here, then, is what these students observed in the war stories of the twentieth century: a progressive abandonment of the world of nature for the world of technology, radical dislocation of relationships between men and women, and the emergence of new attitudes toward religion and spirituality. As they progressed, the students became sensitive to the range of tones through which survivors mediated their experience—in voices ranging from the ironic to the absurd. Thus they were able to make connections between the war experience and the characteristic "voice" of modern humankind.

In many subtle ways, literature conveys values because—or to the extent that—it allows students to reimagine and then to live and experience the images of the text. This act of "entering in" and the transformations of consciousness that accompany it is the essential moral transaction of the literature classroom, I think. My students were susceptible to the particular transformations of war literature because—reflecting the composition of the student body of the college—they were predominantly male, somewhat conventional in their views of reality, conservative, and patriotic. Several were graduates of military high schools, one was a veteran, and all were to some extent consumers of Owen's "old lie." Chivalry moved them; they were capable of being stirred by images of flashing sabres, cavalry charges, and shot-torn flags. Precisely because of this consciousness, they were able to enter into the experience of an idealistic, romantic youth like Henry Fleming or Wilfred Owen. And as time passed, they came to imagine, despite their illusions, what a machine gun could do to a cavalry charge or the consequences of mustard gas.

Conversely, because these students represented some of the better aspects of the white Anglo-Saxon male system, they were able to argue the intrinsic worth of that system, its potential for idealism, honorable service, and transcendence of self. They believed in these values. They had all seen *Chariots of Fire.* Writing their weekly essays on guns and planes, they taught me about the fascinations of war and the male love of tinkering with things that go bang. They reminded me as they wrote about various social systems—home, school, and body politic—that, as one student put it, "a certain amount of mayhem is unavoidable in a competitive culture."

In particular, as they talked about what goes on in schools, a great deal of anger with the system that had nurtured them—or more commonly failed to nurture them—began to emerge. These students were successful and achievement-oriented. They did not vibrate with frustration like Frankie, set fires like Danny, or wear the blank masks of Genna and Greg. Yet they recalled their own schooling as an extended process of humiliation. One young man, who spoke infrequently during the semester, broke a long silence to produce an understatement applauded by all: "The school system does not foster inner peace."

I sometimes became impatient, as I do in society at large, with those students' calm acceptance of violence as a cultural norm, impervious to any number of doses of nonviolent discipline. But there came, as periodically comes in society, an irenic shift. It came in this particular class when, apropos of Stephen Crane, our resident military historian wrote an essay on the Gatling gun. "When they invented this weapon," he observed, "it became possible to kill too many people."

The Gatling gun, from which we could easily draw a historical line to the missile silos in our back yards, became for us a sort of central metaphor. In taking up this weapon, one philosophy major observed, humankind made an Edenic choice, upsetting some precarious state of universal equilibrium. We went over to the side of the machine; we became gun-men. We ceased to be creatures of nature, of a maternal ecosystem. Earlier, it might have been possible to argue (though, since Agincourt, on tenuous ground) that wars had been fought within nature by natural beings; later wars would be fought by robots. Stephen Crane anticipated this dislocation when he described war as the "grinding of an immense and terrible machine . . ." (43). George Lucas confirms the insight for anyone who has cheered the clockwork fighters in *Star Wars.*

To my recollection, none of these students evolved into pacifists. Their final essays reflected, healthily, not my concerns but those that had brought them into class in the first place. The seminarian wrote on loss of faith as a combat experience, quoting from the letters and papers of Wilfred Owen; the Hemingway fan explored the master's style from her perspective as a tutor in the writing center, explaining carefully the similarities and differences between Hemingway's prose and typical freshman syntax; an English major explored *The Waste Land* as war literature, relating its images of rape and vulnerability to the masculine experience of combat. Most of them agreed with Kurt Vonnegut that it is as useless to write an anti-war book as to write an anti-glacier book. But they had learned to *imagine* the glacier. They had been to touch the great death.

More importantly, as they wrestled with ideas, the texts, and each other in writing groups, they had a sort of laboratory experience in conflict and conflict resolution. I make no claim for the uniqueness of my classroom in this respect; indeed, a central point I wish to explore in the next few chapters is that, although we English teachers could perhaps learn something from Woolman, King, Gandhi, or Daniel Berrigan about the theory and practice of nonviolence, we have already learned a great deal from the theorists in our own field who have challenged traditional patterns of classroom interaction.

The Passable Classroom

My image of the centered classroom comes, as any liberal arts major will recognize, from Edward Hicks' famous painting "The Peaceable Kingdom" (actually—and this is not without significance—he painted the scene over and over). Rather like a relentless Bronson Alcott, I try each Monday to set up utopian communities of reflection, acceptance, and useful work. The reality, however, is more perfectly realized in Woody Allen's send-up of Isaiah 11:6–8: "The lion and the calf shall lie down together, but the calf won't get much sleep" (25). On Tuesday, lines form outside my office door.

Tempers have flared in a writing group. Jane feels "put down." Paul has been mocked. Will I please intervene?

I decline the role of fixer, repeating my central maxim: If it happens in the group, deal with it in the group. But I worry a lot. Fighting? In the peaceable kingdom? Edward Hicks, remember, continually revised his kingdom (now a calf, now a lamb). Every year that I teach English I am forced to begin anew, usually at midterm. I get it right, but only for a day, only for these students, only for who I have become this year. And "right" only means faithful to a vision that comes and goes in a mist (now a lamb, now a lion). The revision process roots up layers of self-doubt and buried anger. It inevitably challenges my need to control everything. The classes break down in chaos, then are patiently salvaged and sorted out (not always by me). Every year I learn anew to trust the group, the texts, and some force that through the green fuse drives the flower. Like Edward Hicks, I paint the same general picture, but it comes from a different place in my spirit. Don't ever call me at midterm—I will be very crabby.

In this initial course, tempers had run high, but the quality of the final work had been unusually rewarding. Men had squared off with women, old with young, veterans with draft resisters. They had grappled with hostility and fear. In the end as one student wrote in his final evaluation, "The way the class pulled together as a group was really amazing, something I have never seen quite to this degree. It seemed as though everyone was linked by a common bond which allowed them to speak freely and ultimately resulted in a higher level of learning because of the idea pool."

I look with new eyes at Edward Hicks' painting, seeing for the first time how much tension is balanced and held momentarily static in this image of peacemaking. That is a *lion* there. That baby animal is right in his paws.

In my early days of teaching I think I hoped for a certain docility and gentleness to distinguish our discourse community, but I have come to believe that the literature classroom should be, in a certain sense, dangerous. If it is too placid, I suspect we are not really listening to the texts. The lecture format, of course, protects one from the undertows of one's subject; in my early teaching days I had to cling to the lectern with both hands to control my shaking. For the teacher, it is terrifying to cede control—sometimes to shake in public—and I can't testify that it becomes less terrifying with experience. Yet I believe that by giving students their autonomy we win our own. We expect our students to "change" in the course of a semester. If we ourselves are not changing, I suspect we are not permitting ourselves to be put at risk by our students, by Borges, Kozinski, and Conrad.

The Poem of Force

> Do not mistake the rule of force for true power. Men are not shaped by force.
>
> —Euripedes, *The Bacchae* (19)

> Only he who has measured the dominion of force, and knows how not to respect it, is capable of love and justice.
>
> —Simone Weil, "*The Iliad* or the Poem of Force" (34)

I had gone off to be a teacher, asking myself from time to time if it might be possible to teach English in such a way that people would stop killing each other. As I struggled with professional life, it became more and more clear to me that, indeed, most of our traditional teaching methods feed the purposes of an overweening military, fuel our students' anger, and destroy students' confidence and self-respect—in effect, stunt the very reflective powers that alone make the individual able to resist the dominion of force. War (like grading) is not part of the system, it *is* the system.

We take the adversarial stance for granted; to a certain extent, we thrive on it. There's a prototypic conversation I have about once a year with some student or other who fondly recalls for me his high school days (or his freshman year) and his heroic suffering under some primordial terror of an English teacher: "He really taught me to write," the student will say with the glee of a bootcamp survivor. "He yelled at me. He told me I was a fool. Nothing I did pleased him. I came out of there feeling like a low-life. . . ."

The students with whom I have had this conversation over the years have usually been English majors and teachers-in-training. I'm glad they know how to write, if in fact they do, but I question the style of pedagogy they will pass on in turn. "The villainy you teach me I will execute," says Shylock, "and it shall go hard, but I will better the instruction." Recently I was talking about the use of positive reinforcement in the classroom with an unusually gentle young education major who had quite a lot of teaching experience. Even this kindly, well-disposed young man had to say, "I find it difficult to give my students the affirmation they need. I didn't get it myself as a student. You have to unlearn as a teacher more than you learn."

Most academic brutalization is more subtle than the cases of corporal punishment most of us have come across from time to time. I think, for example, of rude and demoralizing labeling of student work: "Vapid philosophizing," "Execrable grammar," or the pervasive, "HUH?" My point is simply that by being insulted, bullied, and turned into objects, young people learn to insult, bully, and turn others into objects. These actions contain the seeds of violence. It follows, therefore, that the first step in teaching peace is to examine the ways in which we are already teaching conflict.

It works. Punishment works. Violence works, at least in the short term. I guess that's why we keep doing it. It's easy, too, and takes little thought. "It's the only thing they understand." This sentence came to me today as I off-handedly slapped the dog for joyously spreading garbage across the kitchen floor. Our well of folk wisdom justifies quite a lot of casual mayhem.

Violence is easy. Nonviolence, by contrast, takes all we have and costs not less than everything.

A Preliminary Sketch of the Principles

Given the difficulty of the task, the extent of our programming in violence, it's amazing how few students we actually damage. Indeed, if we attempt to examine the writing-and-literature class as an instrument of peacemaking, we find deep-rooted strengths to call upon. First of all, as teachers in the humanities, we encourage students to explore the inner life. Struggling for identity in a materialistic culture, young people run the risk of becoming robots, like Stephen Crane's soldiers, "methodical idiots" and "machinelike fools" (37). In leisure hours students deliver their brains to the Walkman and their hands to the controls of video games. At school they present themselves as passive vessels to be filled by the lecturer; they "interface" with computers, and in a variety of "learning labs" they are willingly plugged in and turned on. At what point do they stumble on an inner life? When do they discover the questions of the heart and the leadings of the intuition? The first goal of education—if we think it has anything at all to do with values—is to bring students to a knowledge of the world within: its geography and anthropology, depths and heights, myths and primary texts. To foster this process, you don't even have to put your chairs in a circle.

Our second goal should be to help the student bring his subjective vision into community, checking his insights against those of allies and adversaries, against the subjective vision of the texts he studies, and in general against the history of ideas. The classroom, then, must be a meeting place for both silent meditation and verbal witness, of interplay between interiority and community.

Certain things we've always done in English class, things that are indeed identified with the structure of our discipline, need to be mediated here as *practice toward the tranquil mind:* writing essays, for example, the time-honored means of helping our students objectify the world within. It's very helpful if the teacher can point out as the course progresses the recurring ideas, images, and patterns in a student's weekly essays, the geography of inner life. It's not necessary or even useful for the teacher to interpret these data. That will be the business of the rest of the student's contemplative life. It is sufficient for a young person to realize that such patterns exist and that his own are different from the traces other writers leave of themselves. As the teacher responds to weekly essays, she can help the student formulate questions, examine the implications of ideas, suggest stylistic improvements, and recommend directions for research.

Obviously, class discussion is also vital to the dialogue between inner life and outer world. It is important that everyone in the class should talk so that discussion is not dominated by the merely extroverted. The teacher needs to develop immediately, before the shy people become typecast, techniques for broadening class discussion. Small groups are excellent for this purpose because they permit the shy student to hear his own voice and build rapport with at least four or five others who will (usually) cheer him on to further discussion. In this context, I think the writing group—as envisioned by contemporary writing theorists—functions specifically as a peacemaking strategy: it encourages us to listen to each other and figure out ways of criticizing without inflicting terminal injury, and it helps us learn to accept criticism without rancor. The writing group forces us to stake out the terrain between our own and other people's view of reality; hence, it reinforces both personal identity and the sense of relationship to a community. It puts authority where it belongs: in whatever is compelling, whatever speaks to the heart and intelligence. I hope, in consequence, it makes for inner peace.

Another aspect of the peaceable classroom implicit in the emphasis on essay and discussion is that it should allow a great deal of interaction between "received information" and student questions: questions generated in essays, short five-minute writings at the beginning of the period, regular brainstorming sessions, etc. At this intersection I would suggest we *do* need to examine our teaching practice. Lecturing is an unlikely way to help students attend to the inner music, nor is the tense exchange that often passes for lecture-discussion. While the well-made lecture has an unassailable place in any curriculum, one must be wary of institutions in which lecture develops as the principal means of conveying information. We have a lot to tell our students, but I believe our primary job should be to bring them to asking, by whatever means we can devise, the questions that will elicit what they need to know. Students do not really listen well to the answers to questions they have not learned to ask.

Finally, no matter what pedagogical approach is used, education for peace must be intellectually challenging. I believe that what T. S. Eliot said about religion ("Thoughts After Lambeth," 329) is true of the life of the mind in general: it will not appeal to young people unless it demands a great deal of them. A class that is not intellectually challenging makes students feel guilty and inadequate. Guilt and inadequacy are the fuel of anger and despair.

When my students tried, as they often did, to apply the insights of war literature to social analysis, trying to figure out how to defuse society, they usually found themselves rearranging traditional categories of Western thought: consensus and authority, cooperation and competition, inner and outer worlds of consciousness, male and female, intuitional and rational, mechanistic and natural. These students would tell me, for example, that our educational system has traditionally emphasized an authoritative, competitive, external, male, rational, mechanistic ordering of reality. Although this system has moved society forward in astonishing ways, they concluded that civilization is now at a point where its very survival depends upon an integration with its lost sister/twin. We need to explore other alternatives. Because our society has traditionally believed that it is good to obey orders and respect superiors, we know a great deal about how authority works. Now we need to find out how consensus works, for it too has its inner laws, stops, and complexities. We know a lot about competition, little about cooperation; more about the male than the female; the outer world than the inner; the rational than the intuitive; the machine than the garden.

"We inhabit a world," observed Alain Renoir, the Berkeley classicist lecturing at Macalester College in 1976, "in which it is more important to have invented the light bulb than to have written the *Seven Against Thebes.*" Our approach to education (as well as to health care, corporate structure, and many other aspects of culture) is predicated on this pragmatic value system. In a different kind of world, we might be sitting in the firelight, chanting heroic verse—though that would not necessarily be better, or even more peaceable. I left my first experiment in peace studies with the most elementary question: could we imagine a different world, a different balance of forces? Imagining, after all, should be what English teachers are best at.

Lying sleepless in bed, listening to the bombs fall on London, Virginia Woolf put the issue more pointedly: "Unless we can think peace into existence we—not this one body in this one bed but millions of bodies yet to be born—will lie in the same darkness and hear the same death rattle overhead" (*Death of a Moth and Other Essays*, 243).

Two

Inner Peace Studies and the World of the Writing Teacher

*W*ould you die for an idea? Should your life, like a good essay, have a thesis? That was what passed for "theory" when I was in graduate school.

In response, I had settled on exploring the idea of nonviolence. And I had done so in a kind of blithe and insouciant mood. Why not? I had been educated to think that life should have a focus. Nonviolence seemed to me a better focus than certain other choices available in 1968. I did not even think nonviolence was an absolute moral imperative—people I respected greatly held contrary views. I rather hoped that the Strategic Air Command would continue to hold contrary views while I worked out my ideas in retired leisure. But I thought, and I still think, that nonviolence is an important experiment, and that certain people have to undertake experiments and live out the consequences of ideas for the benefit of the rest, even if the ideas turn out to be wrong—especially if they turn out to be wrong. I know people who have dedicated their lives to ideas, both foolish and salutary, from open marriage to voluntary poverty, and the consequences have not failed to be interesting to the onlookers.

If we begin with nonviolent theory as an instrument of critical inquiry, though, we may be dismayed by the magnitude of the task, which presents us with nothing less than the warp and woof of Western culture. When you go at life with a question and simply try to follow the trail of answers, then all the familiar contours of culture begin to shift. Everything is connected to everything else, and the web shakes with any touch at its farthest margins.

Having disturbed the web, I was pledged to its net of connection. After teaching "War and the Modern Imagination," I teamed up with a theologian-colleague who wanted to teach a course called "Literature of War/Theology of Peace." Here again we were not trying to accomplish any specific agenda but simply "listening to the texts." We were trying to understand what war is like and what it does to people and what the consequences of that knowledge ought to be for us as students and teachers. Subsequently, my colleague and I went on to teach other courses in the area of social justice because that was the next place our query about violence took us. These classes all combined reading, writing, self-analysis, social analysis, and discussion with a practical focus. We would spend the night with homeless people, make spaghetti in church basements, and so on. Then we would go back to school and talk about what had happened and how we felt, always trying to place the academic readings of the course in a context of our direct experience.

This sort of education can be defined in the broadest sense as "peace studies." Formal peace curricula often focus on questions I think of as the modern equivalent of "How many angels can dance on the head of a pin?" How many missiles do they have? How many do we have? Perhaps what I am encouraging instead is Inner Peace Studies, which asks Who am I? Am I at peace with who I am? Who are these other people? What is the nature of community? What do they believe, and why? Is it possible for us to work together? I am glad I have learned to focus on this latter kind of questioning because, even in my brief experience, missile-counts periodically become irrelevant. Today's headlines tell me, for example, that the world is at peace (oh, well, excluding Eastern Europe) and on the margin of a "new world order." It's proposed, then, that we scale down the military, scale down peace studies. I will let the military make its own arguments, but as for me, I don't believe for a moment that the heart of humankind has changed. I would like to get on with the kind of education that over the course of time *will* change it.

It used to bother me that teaching English seemed irrelevant to people's "real" problems: from babies dying of dysentery in Guatemala to old men sleeping in dumpsters. Every time a national crisis arises, I take, at least in fantasy, the Simone Weil Memorial Plunge into activism. Simone Weil, brilliant philosopher and writer that she was, could seldom resist the urge to get physically involved. Her instinct for solidarity led her to take on the grimmest factory jobs, enlist with the Spanish Loyalists, and so on. Yet frail as she also was, she seemed only to get in the way: to get sick, to fall into the campfire, to burn herself, and to have to be carried home. As would I.

Yet I know that mere good teaching changes things, and those of us who are good at it should do it and not something we might consider more glamorous. This brings us back to the Buddhist concept of right livelihood: "Select a vocation which helps realize your ideal of compassion," as the Vietnamese Buddhist Thich Nh'ât Hanh phrases it (*Being Peace*, 97). Does your daily work contribute to peace and justice or does it not? One doesn't have to eat spaghetti in church basements. One can just teach English. If a single person is, in the Zen sense, awake and present, people wake up all around.

Most of my activist forays have accomplished little, but they have taught me to think about the daily life of teaching. I had begun teaching in 1967, feeling myself to be a robotic arm of the war machine. But only a few years later, composition pedagogy began to change radically with the publication of Ken Macrorie's *Telling Writing* (1970) and Peter Elbow's *Writing Without Teachers* (1972). By incorporating such strategies as group process and freewriting, by defining the concept of voice—what we now think of as a process model for teaching writing—Macrorie, Elbow, and their colleagues were laying out, I believe, a pedagogy of nonviolence. And that is why, in this chapter, I would like to look more closely at our teaching of writing in light of a pacifist discipline.

Recently at an East Coast conference, a young graduate student told me that, really, all of this theorizing about teaching is just a game. "It gives us something to talk about," he said. "None of it means anything." I laughed, mostly out of nervous pique. "Excuse me," I thought, too shy to speak, "but I think this game is a matter of life or death."

Reading the Circle

Perhaps you don't want to take to the streets, you just, like most good teachers, want to play your part in creating a certain kind of human being: compassionate, balanced, and inwardly mobile. In about 1972, a critical mass of freshman composition teachers with this modest agenda (or merely a dumb instinct about what helps students to write better) put their classroom chairs in a circle. The "hundredth monkeys" in this national experiment were, I'm quite sure, my friend Jim Vopat and I, who, one day on the Wisconsin prairie, got hold of Ken Macrorie's *Telling Writing*. That scrape of chairs twenty years ago marked the beginning of a gentle revolution.

Our culture, as anthropologists from other cultures keep trying to tell us, is notably fond of the square, but I do not believe the *New York Times* bothered to report a paradigm shift in 1972, when college teachers began to engage in this fundamentally non-Western act of centering. In his essay, "The Spiritual Legacy of the American Indian," Joseph Epes Brown talks about the importance of one particular symbolic motif in Plains Indian culture, that of the cross within the circle: "At the center of the circle, uniting within a point the cross of the four directions of space and all the other quaternaries of the Universe, is man. Without the awareness that he bears within himself this sacred center, a man is in fact less than man. It is to recall the virtual reality of this center that the Indians have so many rites based on the cross within the circle" (14).

We teachers had begun at some intuitive level to pay attention to this new wisdom about where "man" and even woman move and have their being. We began to discover that as teachers, one of our jobs is to help a student find her "sacred center," the place where she stands at the crossroads of human experience. Beyond that, we needed to help her to see that she exists within another circle: a community. To find voice and to mediate voice in a circle of others is one of the central dialectics of the peaceable classroom.

An architect friend of mine believes that most human problems are, at base, architectural problems. Certainly culture creates spaces that announce the cultural agenda; we can read them like texts. When I went to grammar school we sat in squares of desks bolted to the floor. When I first began to teach I lectured, or engineered the kind of Socratic dialogue that always went exactly where Socrates wanted it to go. If some teachers are doing things differently now, it is not because of a pedagogical fad, but because of a significant shift in our collective goals for the human quest. Small changes in the way we do things have great consequences, especially when they are changes in the way we deal with children and young people. Cradles are different from cribs, and they promote a different future. A baby who is tucked into a stroller and thrust out on rubber wheels among the scurrying legs of shoppers is likely to grow into a different child than the baby who is carried on the breast of its mother or father. When these children, however nurtured, go to school, the classroom will dominate their consciousness for sixteen years or more. Its boundaries will be their boundaries, its possibilities their own.

The arrangement of our classrooms should tell us, if we do not consciously know, what horizon we have set for the next generation. Some twenty years ago, the Brazilian philosopher of education, Paulo Freire, criticized the traditional classroom for its contribution to oppression and depersonalization:

> A careful analysis of the teacher-student relationship at any level, inside or outside of school, reveals its fundamentally narrative character. This relationship involves a narrating Subject (the teacher) and patient, listening Objects (the students). The contents, whether values or empirical dimensions of reality, tend in the process of being narrated to become lifeless and petrified (67).

This "banking method" of education, as Freire calls it, in which the lecturing professor fills the passive student with culture, ensures that little critical thinking will occur. Therefore, he continues, "The educated man is the adapted man, because he is better 'fit' for the world. Translated into practice, this concept is well suited to the purposes of the oppressors, whose tranquillity rests on how well men fit the world the oppressors have created, and how little they question it" (63).

As a young teacher I dug my nails into the lectern and repeated patterns that didn't work for reasons I didn't understand. And that was probably fine because I would have been too stupid and inexperienced to play the kind of fastball you have to play in the truly centered classroom. When people sit around in a group and share experiences, the universe of possibility begins to change. Be it *campesinos* in Guatemala, or household workers in Baltimore, when people sit and tell each other what the world is like for them, the air becomes electric with both danger and hope.

As we roam our classrooms monitoring writing group activity, we can often feel the mood shift as people become seriously engaged. I am thinking about Rod and Clara (two unlikely collaborators) whom I sat watching one day as they vigorously debated in a corner. Since three people happened to be absent from their group, I thought these two would bolt through their critiques and leave in ten minutes, but they were head-to-head for the whole hour. Rod's essay (he was an

ROTC cadet) was about the necessity of U.S. intervention in Latin America. Clara's was about being a brown-skinned child in a white-skinned school. After class Clara said mildly to me, "I like my writing group. You get to know people so well, hearing about their lives from week to week." But it was Rod who wrote a few weeks later, "I can't stand knowing so much about how people really live. How can I make decisions on this basis?"

What a complicated epistemological question, one that underlies much of our cultural valorization of the "objective mode." "Don't argue the hard cases," they told me in moral theology. That means, as I found out in community organizing, don't talk about the particular, concrete, and ludicrous problems people sit with in real life. After such knowledge, what forgiveness?

Back in the days when I clung to the lectern and stuttered about Kierkegaard, it was OK. I transmitted the best Western-human game plan I knew. If Zach didn't get it, that was Zach's problem. If students sit in a classroom and write down what the teacher tells them, they can at least make good, clean theory. Yet when I stopped lecturing it was better. If students have to listen to what other students have to say—and to the teacher, and to Kierkegaard, because I don't want to leave him out—then they have to enter into a kind of dance. They will have to write very complicated theories, or no theory, or a montage of theories. Perhaps I am describing the postmodern sensibility.

It is a dance, but it is not some kind of bagatelle with nothing at stake. At the same conference where I encountered the playful graduate student, I came upon yet another version of Isaiah 11:6–8, this time as the subject of a Fritz Eichenberg woodcut. Eichenburg's animals vibrate with hostility—or is it merely energy? They look ready to pounce. The slit eyes of that panther reminded me of a student I taught last semester. What holds them in the light? It's a mystery to me. An uncontrollable mystery.

Freewriting the Future

Keep thy heart in all diligence, for out of it are the issues of life.

—Proverbs 4:23

There is that near you which will guide you; O! wait for it and be sure ye keep to it . . .

—Isaac Penington (155)

A second tool of nonviolent discipline in the writing class is freewriting (as most teachers call it). Others speak of automatic writing (with its nostalgic overlay of 1920's psychic experiments), or "shot-gun writing" (a metaphor not entirely compatible with the pacifist analysis). In our department we call it "prewriting," because we like to emphasize that it is not a final product but a first stage in generating material.

"Automatic writing" has been something many writers throughout literary history have practiced or fallen into in one altered state or another. Writers have always sensed the need to invite something outside consciousness to overcome their ego in order to push past the boundaries of analytical thought: muse, *daimonos*, or some picturesque entity channeled from another and presumably more articulate age. Freudian free-association is an immediate antecedent and, more popularly, the burgeoning science of group dynamics with its "brainstorming" methodologies. But it was (again) Ken Macrorie who in 1970, gave most of us the famous advice to "write for ten minutes as fast as you can, never stopping to ponder a thought. Put down whatever comes to your mind . . ." (18).

Usually when I introduce prewriting to new students, I have them practice in class with a couple of topics; almost anything will do ("The Worst Teacher I Ever Had" usually generates a lot of passion). When students report back on the experience, they often mention how surprised they were that they had so much to say on a topic. Often, too, they are pleased with the good ideas that seem to come out of nowhere or the nice turns of phrase that surprise even the reluctant writer.

In general, I think we've discovered that there are four advantages of prewriting:

1. It helps us to get started. Fear of the blank page is probably the single biggest obstacle to writing.
2. It helps us to discover connections between ideas that we might never get to if we tried to reason out the problem step by step. Writing used to be taught as a predominantly logical process: you go from A to B to C—outlining, indeed, asks us to do precisely that. And C is a good place to get to but may be a boring place to stop: unsatisfying for reader and writer. Like that relentless logician, Mr. Ramsay in *To the Lighthouse*, we want to get to Q. Prewriting can often get us to Q by an intuitive leap. What prewriting strategies do, then, is help us to call forth contemplative resources we seldom use.
3. It helps us to find subjects or tells us when we don't have a subject. The subject, indeed, might be "Q." Many students who master the basics of composition bore themselves and their teachers by never having anything interesting or thoughtful to say. Prewriting can often lead to a new idea worth exploring.
4. It helps us to write in a natural voice—a voice often deadened by compulsive editing too early in the process.

Years of schooling, years of social pressures, turn most writers into generic products, neatly wrapped in yellow and black. Like Auden's "Unknown Citizen," we develop the proper opinions for our age and ethnic group. We write the generic theme and get generic comments from the generic teacher. We become Freire's "adapted" men and women. Is this worth our lives? In prewriting, by contrast, we begin to listen to voices inside. They may surprise us. They may surprise the world, which badly needs new ideas.

For Macrorie and his dharma heirs, freewriting was a way of gaining access to the natural reservoirs of language all students possess, dammed up, in so many, by inflexible methods of child rearing and education. However much he talks about the practical problems of writing, though, Macrorie's focus is implicitly moral. "Truth" is one of his favorite words. Opening the third edition of *Telling Writing* at random, I chance on page fifteen where, after starting with a quotation from a journalist named Gene Baro ("He told the truth in order to see,") Macrorie subtitles the chapter "Telling Truths." He then opens with the righteous sentence, "All good writers speak in honest voices and tell the truth," quotes Eudora Welty in support of his position, and winds up recommending that a good writer should first "shake the habit" of telling lies. This pedagogy has a moral basis; why didn't somebody sue him?

The contemporary approach to teaching writing, may I repeat, was developed in the shadow of the Vietnam experience by people listening, perhaps more carefully than usual, for lies.

Where Macrorie (and I and those of our ilk) may be faulted is in our underlying presumption that *it is a good thing* to encourage an expression of the inner world. I know that some of my colleagues, for various reasons, believe it is *not* a good thing. One of them bluntly asserts that she does not want to know anything about students that can't be graded on a computer. Others think that "personal writing" verges on psychoanalysis, and they are not comfortable with any blurring of professional lines. It's reasonable to recognize that, underlying process theory, is a somewhat idealistic, Whitmanesque premise. It's fair to say, too, that those of us who are attracted to these philosophies probably share an interest in both personal liberation and sympathetic identification with other people: the two seem to me intimately connected. I do not apologize for this position but merely issue a consumer warning. I've been a college teacher for twenty-two years, and, besides, I've taught writing process in contexts as diverse as religious communities and shelters for the chronically mentally ill and alcoholic. I've taught freewriting to people who were drunk, drooling, and carrying weapons. In all that time, I've only seen two pieces of writing that seemed to me dangerously violent or perverse (both were from upper middle class college students).

But it's always well to take a trip to the famous dark side. In fact, when I first learned about freewriting I had a lot of objections to it, which were based on a poorly understood Freudian model of the unconscious that I carried at the time. I was afraid that freewriting might pull up dark memories and trauma for certain students, turning English class into some kind of therapy session. ("Some kind of therapy session": now why do we use that phrase in a pejorative sense—as though we do not need all the help we can get?)

But in any case, the buried wrecks of consciousness seldom surface in my class. (I have noticed that teachers get what they want to get; some people love to hear about the psychological level of student life, and they do hear it. I crave stories about intellectual struggle, principalities and powers, wrestling matches with angels that leave us limping—and I seem to get students who are predisposed to tell me such tales. There is no pre-selection process at work here: our academic computers, I guess, are tuned in to the finer currents of the universe.) Anyway, it's hard for me to remember how strongly I objected to prewriting at first. Perhaps my reservations had more to say about my own inner world than that of my students. I didn't keep a journal in those days, and, even when I began to do so, I had trouble being truthful (as Macrorie would recommend); the first year's entries in my prewriting journal could have been inscribed, like a sundial, "Count Only the Happy Hours."

Later, as I became more committed to the process, I learned to open myself more to painful feelings and confusion. I found that the act of externalizing and owning up to confused feelings can give one a measure of equilibrium. Slowly, my paradigm of the unconscious changed; I began to sense that inner space was deeper and wider than I had supposed; it was benevolent and unconstricted. Thus it occurs to me that what we do in daily, free, surrendered writing is very much like Zen practice, and by means of it we come to something Zen teachers call "great mind" or "the larger container," a place of focused and compassionate clarity.

Students seem to go on a similar journey, and I think we can trust them to do it, although all of us need teachers, help, and fellowship on the way. Fortunately, at my university we have excellent counselling services, and I'm grateful for that back-up. But in the main, freewriting seems to be self-correcting and, at its best, self-healing. No one, to my knowledge, has begun channeling Shirley MacLaine.

I would like to meet the concern about turning the classroom into "some kind of therapy group," then, by observing that good teaching *is*, in the classical sense, therapy: good teaching involves reweaving the spirit. (Bad teaching, by contrast, is soul murder.) If we compare teaching English merely to traditional psychoanalysis, only one of the many healing arts, we find interesting parallels. An analyst listens to a client with the same questions in mind that a literary scholar asks of a text: What recurs? What is emphasized? Why this word and not that? What is the meaning of this pattern of images? These parallels are not surprising since Freud borrowed much of his methodology from creative writers.

In general, I find it more productive to look at how things (like teaching writing and doing therapy) are similar, rather than at how they are, and thus should remain, different. Rather than retreating from the therapy analogy, I suggest we focus on it to see what it has to tell us. It tells me that we need a great deal of psychological and spiritual insight in order to do our teaching jobs properly, an understanding conveyed primarily in the depth of our listening. Most of the healing that goes on in English class (and maybe everywhere) is self-healing. The teacher's job is not so much to counsel as to provide an atmosphere of safety and to keep out of the way of the process.

The Cordelia School of Writing Pedagogy

> Unless you feel it, you will never achieve it.
> If it doesn't flow from your soul
> With natural, easy power,
> Your listeners will not believe it.
>
> —Goethe, *Faust* (161)

Once I had a violin teacher who stopped me every couple of notes to offer her critique. She was a brilliant musician, but, for me, a terrible teacher. After a while I learned to stop *myself.* Play a few notes. Stop. I learned to project a little critic-puppet outside my own brain whose favorite word was *wrong*! This way I could keep my crabby teacher with me always, even in the privacy of practice. My teacher had been trained in a Hungarian conservatory and had the scars to prove it; literally, her neck was scored and scabbed where the violin's chin rest met her flesh. I have a new teacher now, whose habit is to stand somewhere behind me in the lesson room as I play. She never says "That was right," as though she looked through God's eyes, but rather "I enjoyed your approach there." She will ask me why I'm playing a slur "that way" and we will talk about the options. But her comments are brief, and, since she declines to give me constant feedback, I am learning to listen to myself. Above all, she keeps me moving, practicing, turning the pages.

If we can get our students to listen to what they are doing, we will have taught them a great deal. Yet I make these suggestions about classroom practice with great trepidation because we as teachers have so long evaluated ourselves on conscientiously "correcting" every single student mistake. Teaching English (in particular) has become a branch of the police. (I have this, and more, in common with my cousin in the LAPD.) Consequently, we can hardly go to a cocktail party without spreading a plague of tongue-tied grammar-anxiety. Though Mina Shaughnessy, in 1977, made her classic case against over-policing student error, many of us still define our success as teachers by our skill at "marking," as the British say. Such an approach to teaching inhibits students' ability to find their own strength.

Even our positive responses often merely addict students to repeating their most successful tricks. Both praise and blame set students looking to other people for definitions of the self. Both discourage creative problem solving because you can't solve problems in new ways when you have an eye on what "they" might think. (YOU are THEY, we need to tell ourselves and our students.)

What, then, am I recommending? That we do nothing, say nothing: the Cordelia School of Writing Pedagogy? Well, indeed, I think most of us could say a lot less. But I am recommending, above all, that we pay attention; if we pay attention, then each of us in a given situation will soon know how much is too much. I'm suggesting that we shift our sense of ourselves as successful teachers away from the quality of our corrections and toward the quality of our mindfulness. I do not know why the act of paying acute attention changes the dynamics of a situation, but I can say without reservation that it does. Buddhists know a lot about this, but in the interests of multiculturalism, I will quote Tolstoy on the subject: "Now! It is the most important time because it is the only time when we have any power" (298). The most important person, he goes on to say, is the person we are with, for who knows if we will have dealings with anyone else?

I think we can count it a good teaching year when we do not actually make a number of students *stop* doing whatever it is we teach. (Frequently, teachers manage to make certain students stop doing all academic tasks as early as first grade.) It might help to think about the things each of us has stopped doing: dancing? singing? making art? These are all natural human activities, accessible to everyone.

On the other hand, if we have kept students turning the pages and practicing, call it a good year. For it is, as Annie Dillard says, the page that teaches you to write:

> The page, the page, that eternal blankness, the blankness of eternity which you cover slowly, affirming time's scrawl as a right and your daring as necessity; the page, which you cover woodenly, ruining it, but asserting your freedom and power to act, acknowledging that you ruin everything you touch but touching it nevertheless, because acting is better than being here in mere opacity; the page . . . (58–59).

Now the Cordelia School of Writing Pedagogy may not seem sufficiently *rigorous*, that focus so curiously shared by teachers and morticians. And I am going to resist my puritanical tendency to tell you that it *is* in fact hard. On the contrary, most things that flow from the heart's true center have a certain ease to them: this is a sign that we have found our life's perfect work. Instead let me return to the studio of my Hungarian violin teacher. I do not want to paint her as a termagant. She had a generous, giving heart, and I could not help but love her. By the end of my lesson, she would be rank with sweat. She would lose all sense of time and rant into the next student's hour, correcting, badgering, fussing with details in her caring and hopeless way. Then, too, I worried about her: the sores on her neck would fester on my behalf. For her, I practiced until I injured my hands. (But what did we get through that year? One or two bits of Boccherini and Beethoven that I will never play again because I can't play them "right.")

At the end of the day, surely that scarred woman knew she had *worked*, she had not wallowed. And many of us similarly judge our effectiveness by the quality of our stigmata.

There are many reasons why I think we should stop abusing ourselves this way—it doesn't help students (especially beginners) learn, it ruins our health and causes us to have colorful breakdowns—but the most important reason is that it ultimately makes us hate students. Lots of teachers hate students, for reasons that have to do with the disproportion between what we put out and what they take in: a disproportion so great that surely, we think, it can only be the result of the students' malice.

I began this digression by talking about creating an atmosphere of safety and then getting out of the way of the process. I will end by repeating that the best thing we can provide is deep, mindful listening. If you think this is too easy, let me reassure you that it takes tremendous concentration; it requires the humility and self-effacement that mark any holy process. That's hard. It's impossible all too much of the time for me.

None of us needs an M.A. in Social Work in order to listen attentively, but we do need many things we probably don't pay enough attention to: an inner life, a high degree of consciousness and intentionality, good discernment, the love of friends, and grounding in some tradition of values.

These are the supports that help us make those wise and lucid comments that keep a writing conference moving: "Excuse me? "Uh huh," etc. And things like, "I wonder why that pattern keeps coming up?" "That little place in the second paragraph really jumps out at me." I often have to fight my tendency to lecture and answer the questions a student's text seems to be raising, an intervention that is usually counterproductive. There are many questions, as Rilke says, that simply must be lived.

Knowing that we encroach on sacred space when we teach prewriting, I think most of us instinctively emphasize the privacy of the process. Students can't (and shouldn't) get very deeply into the inner world if someone is always looking over their shoulders. Therefore, most of us usually pair freewriting with some kind of "focus" exercise that allows the writer to revisit the material, shape, amplify, cut, explain, and edit. Only then is it time to bring it to an audience. Thus, we teach both appropriate sharing and appropriate restraint. As teachers and learners, we come to understand, I hope, what a community can give us and what we can give a community. We learn to give and to hold back: "keeping your heart" does not require you to wear it on your sleeve. This process is, in the classical sense, therapeutic, like going to the oracle at Delphi and talking to the helpers about your dreams.

The philosophy described here may seem like a small thing, a minor adjustment in the humble trade of teaching on this Class-M planet. But I want to suggest, once again, that the things we do in the classroom are not morally neutral. When we taught "the old way," we would tell our students to, in effect, go home, lock the door, take in a lot of caffeine, and produce five hundred words on the life cycle of some Australian mammal; when we did that, we were shaping a certain kind of intellectual life. If we, by contrast, respect the inner world of the student, try to help her gain access to it and to express it with power and authority to a community of listeners, we are crafting a different future.

Choose Life

If you ask students what good writing is, they will give you this kind of analysis:

GOOD WRITING IS:

1. well organized.
2. logical.
3. technically correct in terms of grammar, spelling, and so on.

If you ask them, on the other hand, what they *like to read*, they will tell you something a bit different, and they will have more fun telling you:

GOOD WRITING:

1. tells me something new.
2. builds, goes somewhere, keeps me reading.
3. is funny, or sad, or engages my mind with an idea.
4. gets to the point, doesn't waste words.

The two lists, of course, are not mutually exclusive. To engage my mind, a writer ought to do me the courtesy of presenting ideas in a logical fashion; if he's going to make me laugh, he should try not to destroy the pace with misspellings and grammatical eccentricities.

But most students think that editing functions—ordering, outlining, correcting, and so forth—are more central to good writing than is content. Or at least they think these functions are important to English teachers, and so they try to give us what we want. By contrast, a few mavericks will inevitably comment that some mythic history teacher "only grades on your ideas," as though this were a sign of superior sensibility.

Students have trouble understanding that *writing is thought*, with all the problems of thought. They have trouble understanding that writing is like one of those old-time cowboy movies where the hero stands up on the buckboard and tries to drive two unruly horses called Intuition and Reason. Life, says E. M. Forster in *Howard's End*, demands that we connect the prose and the poetry. That's one of its difficulties, and one reason the peaceable classroom is dangerous: "Life is indeed dangerous, but not in the way morality would have us believe. It is indeed unmanageable, but the essence of it is not a battle. It is unmanageable because it is a romance. . ." (107).

Though process pedagogies are sometimes dismissed as "romantic," I take the epithet as a compliment (for Romanticism almost invariably has implied a concern for inclusivity and social justice). I used to settle for "prose" in Forster's sense from my students. I thought it was unfair to expect young people to be both grammatical and throbbing with life. If a paper was well-organized and technically correct, I would give it a "C," suggesting, without much hope, that in the future the student might try to be more interesting and thoughtful.

Students used to ask, "What do you have to do to get an 'A' in here?" And I would say, as Diaghilev told his dancers, "Etonne-moi."

Since then I have realized, or remembered, that *astonishing each other* is what young people are best at. It is, after all, how they get dates. The writing group is a social transaction, and social exchange rolls along on storytelling, jokes, and something serious to think about. Why should school be different? This is how Augustine in the *Confessions* recalls *his* rhetoric class:

> . . . to talk and laugh and do kindnesses to each other; to read pleasant books together; to make jokes and then talk seriously together; sometimes to disagree, but without any ill feeling, . . . to be sometimes teaching and sometimes learning; to long impatiently for the absent and to welcome them with joy when they return to us . . . (78).

Augustine remembers "the feeling. . . . the face, the voice, the eyes" of his friends, and calls the image "a kindling fire to melt our souls together and out of many to make us one" (78).

Why should school be any less than that? Anything less is not worth our lives.

How many of us look back on our school days as endless torture by exquisite boredom? I do. I look back on my early years of correcting papers with the same sensation.

I'm not willing to put up with that any more. "And these are those poor dead who never were alive," I used to say (of myself and my students) while moving from Dante to sophomore essays on a warm fall afternoon. My friend Jim Vopat, being more liberated, would simply throw them away. "If they're boring, throw them away," he'd say. That's a better comment than a grade. That's a real-world comment. But I was never brave enough. I would drag those manila folders around, as Marley's ghost dragged his cashboxes: "the chains I forged in life."

In the last few years, at first a little diffidently, I have learned to say, "Etonne-moi" right up front; on the first essay, not the third. I tell students that my major goal in teaching is to keep myself enchanted, and that their goal in writing should be the same. I am rewarded (sometimes) with funny essays, sad essays, bizarre ideas that keep me thinking and learning. When we teach students to discover rather than merely to push information around, we are developing writers, not technicians. The most unlikely and reluctant discover, to their astonishment, that they enjoy writing, that they have a flair. If a student writes naturally, in her own voice, she is almost inevitably interesting and thoughtful. It's when we are posturing and hiding and dissembling that we bore others. "Voice" alone cannot sustain a life's work—or even an essay—but it gives us courage and joy and a feeling of authority that sustain us through the discipline of learning the rest of what we need to know.

"RESIST DOING THINGS THAT HAVE NO MEANING FOR LIFE" says the poster over my desk, quoting Pablo Casals. You can get the poster from the Northern Sun Alliance Poster Collective, 1519 Franklin Ave., Minneapolis, MN. I hope they sell out.

It's because I'm trying to be on the side of life that I do not believe in teaching beginning students to write a formal academic dialect, that to do so is to disable them emotionally. We may think that American teachers are perhaps not so ruthless about this as are their European colleagues. In England or France it's still pretty common to send a dialect-speaking student off to the language lab to acquire the proper upper-class intonation; if your educational goal is to raise yourself a step or two in the social system, I suppose this is all to the good, but you may do so at the price of profound alienation from the social supports that keep humans intact.

The American agenda is not so open because we like to pretend there is no class system in America. And because the middle class is so large and dominant, the degradation of voice we practice is more vulgar. We do not try to teach students a civil tongue (to which I would have no objection) but rather some hideous in-group jargon. Too many of us teachers speak (and therefore pass on) the gabble of sociology or education, one of the new Derridean dialects, or a lumpy Feminism. Depending on their intelligence, musical ear, or level of desperation, students do or do not learn to sound like us. The more crafty among them will argue, parroting a professorial opinion, that technical vocabulary is essential to every trade. Because I teach a lot of theology students, I like to tell them that if Jesus had talked like that, he would never have made it out of Nazareth.

Students who have learned to chatter this way often *know* very little; they have substituted mastery of vocabulary for assimilation of ideas. Most students, however, do not learn it, for there is not really time; they do a bad job of mastering the academic style, and their self-esteem suffers along with their prose. They have the native ability to write honest and even elegant English sentences in a simple and straightforward style, but instead they write impenetrable, boring foolishness. They can't master BULL, as William G. Perry put it in his oft-quoted essay so they write COW (227). It does not please the teacher, and the student can feel no pride.

Hearing Voices

By contrast, let us explore a way of teaching that begins by valuing the hoard of words a student brings to class.

One of the first things that happened when we started doing prewriting exercises with students—and when we started doing them ourselves—is that we started hearing voices. In our own journals and in what we heard students reading to each other in their writing groups, we began to hear people talking in a new way, more conversationally, more honestly, more connectedly. That is, with a connection between the written word and the person.

When I talk about "voice" with students, I often feel I am knocking on their prose, saying, "Who's in there? Is anybody home?" More and more often these days somebody is.

Of course, most of us seem to have ingested censorship with our mother's milk or, more likely, with our Similac. "You can't do it that way," I hear someone in a writing group say.

Sentences beginning "you can't" always interest me, so I scurry across the room.

"Tell me why you think he can't do it that way."

"It's too informal, too, um, real. I mean, he says, 'My smile kinda dribbled off my face,' and I think he should say, 'My expression changed radically,' or something. And besides, you can't write *kinda*. It's not correct."

Another student, who plays drums after school in a rock band, says, "Yeah but I like the sound of those two long 'i's' in *kinda* and *smile* and even if you said, 'kind of', it would mess up the rhythm."

"But he's writing this for Professor Paperweight, and Professor Paperweight wants it to be correct."

This type of exchange brings up many of the central issues connected with voice. First of all, we recognize that it's *there*. As teachers we need to affirm that authentic presence and respect the spirit flowing through a student's writing. When a student lets you—and himself—see who he is, in his own words, that important moment needs at least a nod: "OK. Julie is right. You have a great instinct for rhythm and pacing. Keep listening to that in your writing."

But we are not merely in the business of encouraging eccentric genius. We have to help people live with each other. We need to help them find not only voice but a range of voices to mediate their experience in different communities of meaning (including the academic). In affirming the value of home-town talk, we should also recognize that most humans are capable of mastering a number of dialects. "But Jim is right, too. We have an audience problem. Suppose you hand this to Professor Paperweight, just as it is—"

"But if I flunk that class it screws up my average for veterinary school."

"Right, OK. You have some choices."

"Maybe I'll keep my *dribble* and give him his *kind of*. Or maybe I'll cut out *kinda* and just *dribble*. . ."

Giving choices, explaining a variety of strategies and their consequences, is essential to mediating the peaceable classroom. This takes time and sensitivity to people. It's easier to say, "There's no such word as *kinda*."

But finding voice—let's be clear—is a political act. It defines a moment of presence, of being awake; and it involves not only self-understanding, but the ability to transmit that self-understanding to others. Learning to write so that you will be read, therefore, vitalizes both the self and the community. Voiceless writing, as Peter Elbow has observed, drains the reader; writing that has a voice in it gives energy ("The Pleasures of Voice" 212). Perhaps scientists will someday discover that it quickens our heartbeat and warms the extremities. By contrast, as Elbow has also noted, to experience yourself as "voiceless" is a definition of depression, subjugation, and being counted out (221). To "have a voice" is to have authority.

The other day as I was reading the first chapter of Mark's gospel, I came upon the familiar passage where Jesus begins his career of teaching and driving out demons. "He has authority," the people say. "He doesn't talk like the Scribes."

The next question I had to ask was, "How did the Scribes talk?"

Well, I suppose nowadays we would call it "academic discourse."

What Does This Have to do with Nonviolence?

So far in this chapter I have been talking about sharing insight, encouraging the play of intuition as well as critical reflection, and affirming the person by encouraging personal writing. I could tell you about the astonishing things I have learned this semester from student writing: that somebody's father runs around the kitchen every morning, clucking like a hen, pretending to lay the breakfast eggs; that old ladies in Guyana like to trade their needlework for "valiums;" that somebody's grandfather carved Christ's entrance into

Jerusalem, donkey and all, on a garden squash; that when you are kicked by your father at the base of the spine, it feels something like hitting the "crazy bone" of your elbow. I could tell you these things and more, things more interesting than you can see on TV, but what would that have to do with nonviolence?

Oh, war begins in banality, the suppression of the personal and idiosyncratic. By contrast, "A language that takes our emotions seriously and gives them real weight in our lives encourages us to think and be and act differently" (84), writes Dorothee Soelle, the German theologian, who speaks from the shadow of the Holocaust. Coming to America, Soelle was surprised to discover that "at Harvard . . . the first thing they learn is not to say 'I.' That is forbidden. . . . In learning the language of domination, these students learn to give up their subjectivity, their emotionality, their range of experience, their partisanship" (85). Such education feeds the purposes of authoritarian structures, governmental or religious, Soelle goes on to say, fostering "a compulsive need for order, a fear of confusion and chaos, a desire for clarity and control" (110). Finally, she reminds us "The Milgram experiment showed that a vast majority of the ordinary people included in the research were quite prepared, under scientific direction, to torture innocent fellow humans with electric current, which is precisely what happens in a 'culture' of obedience" (111).

Alice Miller, in another post-Holocaust analysis, agrees, saying that "Our capacity to resist has nothing to do with our intelligence but with the degree of access to our true self" (43).

The connections between language and war, between language and oppression, are multiple and complex. Certainly the wars of the twentieth century changed the voice of modern humankind, as we discovered in my first peace studies class—discovering, merely, a truism of linguistics. The voice changed, first because consciousness changed. Truth, they say, is war's first casualty, but so, conversely, are cant and hypocrisy, at least in the world of those under fire. Hemingway's famous declaration on this subject occurs in *A Farewell to Arms:* "I was always embarrassed by the words sacred, glorious, and sacrifice and the expression in vain" (184). The broken, the abused, the dying, cannot bear linguistic hype. The soldier cannot abide any abstraction that denies the particulars of his pain: "There were many words that you could not stand to hear and finally only the names of places had dignity" (185).

Abstractions are useful, particularly in manipulating broad areas of cultural consensus. But before we buy into an abstraction, we need to know what *we* think, or else we put ourselves in danger of becoming the playthings of oppression and mass hysteria. Even when we know what we think, it's hard to resist the roar of the crowd. This was true in World War I, when recruiting posters set before young men the alluring myth of the Arthurian quest, and it was even more true in the Gulf War, when the appropriate level of doublespeak was simply injected intravenously into those of us hooked up to CNN. (Television sets appeared miraculously everywhere at my university during the Gulf War, mounted in the corridors on those wall systems devised to keep hospital patients at rest. And they remain in place.) Now, I do not think that repeating the names of places, along with "certain numbers . . . certain dates" represents any triumph of voice. Rather, the reverse: Hemingway described the depersonalization of men bludgeoned to psychic death by their war experience. But people reach this point of despair because, among other reasons, they have entered mindlessly into a dialect of abstraction, because they have succumbed to a linguistic order that will betray them in the end. This is the essence of "recruitment."

Thus, I have come to distrust any pedagogy that does not begin in the personal. To teach beginning students to write a formal, academic dialect is to disable them not only emotionally but also politically. Having made people feel like charlatans, it submits them, half-clad in rags of personhood, bashful and confused, to the dominion of force.

Of course, a student's inner world may be positively poisonous; she may need to be led away from it toward health and sanity and the laws of physics. Thus, I have come to distrust any pedagogy that does not conclude in the communal: subject to the checks and balances of the others, the teacher, the tradition, and the texts.

Voice and Authority

> The really moving thing in the work of education is listening to a person at the deepest level while preserving round all that he confides us of himself a halo of mystery, patience, care and love, thanks to which, sometimes, we can free him from what he is and give him access to his future.
>
> —Louis Evely (78)

All true political acts are speech acts, Hannah Arendt has written; brute force has no meaning; inarticulateness has no meaning. This is not a perfect analysis from my point of view because silence is, in a sense, "readable"—a point I shall come back to later. But for the moment, let us look more closely at the political importance of art. Someone once said that tyranny does not so much fear guns and tanks as it fears some drunken poet on a barstool who strikes on a phrase to capture the common imagination. Tyranny, face it, fears very few literary critics. There are Irish stories—I do not know if they are historically accurate—about solving boundary disputes with dancing contests. I have heard, too, that rival kings would set their court poets to versify against each other instead of committing the troops to battle. In those days, the poets were second in authority to the high king, or so I have been told.

Finding voice is a spiritual event. In many religious traditions, it is the reward of a vision quest. Think of Isaiah, think of Caedmon, *given words.* And spiritual events change the face of community. A prophet, or a prophetic writer, calls us to a higher standard of what we could be. That's simply a prophet's job description.

This morning I had breakfast with a rural social worker from Zimbabwe. In the villages he serves, the women walk about ten kilometres each morning to fetch water. The children often faint in school because they have had nothing to eat, but more important is the constant longing for enough to drink; even in a culture of hospitality, you begin to begrudge a thirsty traveler.

After this encounter, once again I have to ask, Why teach English? If we don't have a good answer to that question, there is lots to do elsewhere in the world or down the back streets of our cities. My answer for today is that finding voice is a socially-responsible political act. We don't just do it for ourselves. And helping someone to find voice demands a spiritual partnership with that seeker. It's an exercise of compassion. We touch the lives of hundreds of students a year; perhaps one of them will help to figure out a better way to dig irrigation ditches. We can, I hope, give our students a dream of what they can accomplish as *who they are*, in their own right. This requires a special kind of dreaming, the kind Howard Thurman, Martin Luther King's mentor, used to speak of as a great dream we try to waken into.

But not everybody at my university is happy with the present vogue for putting the classroom chairs in a circle. (One professor, for example, is always leaving notes on the board for the janitor: "Tom, NEVER move these chairs.") Such people often want to know—and it's a good question—who's in charge here? Where is the center of authority?

Sometimes it happens in the middle of a writing group session that a certain kind of listening silence falls. As one student goes on reading to her group, the others become voluntarily still. She hears the silence and clutches, or smiles bashfully, but she goes on. *A single compelling voice:* this is at least one locus of authority in the peaceable classroom.

Affirming this insight, Václav Havel's recent political writing would turn us away from a purely "objective" interpretation of reality toward an affirmation of feeling and gut sense—what Blaise Pascal would have called *le coeur* or *le sens intime.* In describing the qualities necessary for survival in the post-modern political world—listen—is Havel not describing our classrooms?

> We must try harder to understand than to explain. The way forward is not in the mere construction of universal systemic solutions, to be applied to reality from the outside; it is also in seeking to get to the heart of reality through personal experience. Such an approach promotes an atmosphere of tolerant solidarity and unity in diversity based on mutual respect, genuine pluralism and parallelism. In a word, human uniqueness, human action and the human spirit must be rehabilitated (15).

Three

"Exterminate . . . The Brutes" and Other Notes Toward a Spirituality of Teaching

*O*ne year, I discovered that I had begun to hate students. It came upon me while I was trying to pull together a conference paper on student-centered teaching (as we called it then). That year, I had a class of twenty-four freshmen who were stonewalling me day after day. Rather like a Victorian cleric with Doubts, I preached to myself the gospel according to Ken Macrorie, while English 102 sat silent, resistant, glowering: an implacable force brooding over an inscrutable intention, as Joseph Conrad (whom I was teaching in senior seminar) might have put it.

Is it any wonder that while writing up my conference proposal I should scrawl across the top of it, like Mr. Kurtz under similar pressure, "Exterminate all the brutes"? This was the phrase I was mumbling under my breath as my younger and presumably more idealistic colleagues talked about what was going on in their classrooms. And I began to think more and more, as one does when one has committed oneself to writing a paper about it, of Mr. Kurtz as a prototype of the writing teacher. Indeed, the Heart of Darkness strikes me as an approporiate metaphor for the classroom in more ways than one. It's here we confront chaos and misrule, savage silence, chills, fever, and, at least in some places where I've taught, failure of the air conditioning.

Mr. Kurtz, like so many of us, begins as an idealist. He writes his manifesto about bringing light and sanitation into the jungle, rather along the lines of Mina Shaughnessy. But he winds up shrinking heads. He acquires a taste for unspeakable acts. I had begun to wonder about the process by which an idealist becomes a cynic. I wondered because, there in English 102, were some heads I was longing to put on stakes outside my office.

In an attempt to understand what was going on, I began to tell all my younger colleagues how we got here, like an old yenta, whether they wanted to know or not. Long ago, I would tell the education majors in my Advanced Writing class, we did not put chairs in a circle as we do now. We taught people in what you might call a sort of missionary position. Now, what happens, I would ask them, if you put your chairs in a circle. Can we make this an experiment in semiotics?

They told me, your attitude toward authority is different. Information is coming from all sides, not just from the front. You are in a cocoon-shape, nest shape, mandala, they said, which feels different from being in a square or a wedge. "You march in a square," said one graduate of a local military high school. "You fight in a square."

They had gotten the point, I guess, or some kind of point. In the centered classroom we're not just teaching people to write, but we are nurturing new social structures and ways of seeing the world—whether or not that is our conscious intent.

Attending professional conferences in the last few years, I've noticed that young people in the profession know rather little about the history of what to some of us in mid-career is still "the new pedagogy"—especially those young people who are trying to critique it. I resolved to answer in my conference paper the question we often ask ourselves in the classroom, "How did I get here?" I proposed to do so by reviewing a few major documents in the revolution such as

Jerry Farber's essay, "The Student as Nigger," which many of us as teaching assistants passed around to each other hot off the ditto machine in 1967.

I hadn't read Jerry Farber's essay in years when I went looking for it, although I did manage to retrieve an old, blue-smudged copy from my files. When I started teaching at the University of Wisconsin-Milwaukee in 1967, I was given a copy of McCrimmon's *Writing With a Purpose* and the advice to "stay out of their sticky little lives." My mother, who taught high school, gave me three ladylike suits and told me not to smile until Christmas. This was what I had in the way of educational methods, philosophy and props—and, as I said earlier, the stakes were high.

There I would be at 7:15 in the morning, trying my best to get across the fine points of "Shooting an Elephant" to students from Polish-speaking families just off the dawn shift at Allis Chalmers. Across the hall one of my colleagues would be sitting cross-legged on his desk chanting "Om." He was the one who slipped me a copy of "The Student as Nigger."

The essay has had what you might call an interesting publishing history. It first appeared in the *Los Angeles Free Press* and was widely reprinted in underground newspapers across the country, in several magazines, and, finally, in a book of the same title. One critic called it a "suppurating sore in the body politic (Farber,14)"; other commentators said it was a "dirty, filthy source of moral poison" and "obscene pornographic smut" (14). No wonder we lined up at the ditto machine.

Farber made the mistake, perhaps, of allowing a metaphor, in this case a sexual one—no one seemed to mind the racial one at the time—to overpower the message he was trying to get across. He compared the classroom transaction to sexual acts I couldn't even pronounce, which, to say the least, alienated a portion of his audience. Or perhaps it wasn't a mistake: the thing certainly got around, it got attention, it was remembered. One administrator I know still quotes it as an example of the degeneracy of all of us who went to graduate school in the 1960s.

As I revisit Farber's essay, though, skimming off the rhetorical excesses as I guess I'd better, I'm struck by its relevance to issues we're still struggling with. He didn't like classroom desks bolted to the floor; he thought grades were lethal weapons in the hands of those too cowardly to fight like men. (Women didn't enter in back then.) Most importantly, he emphasized that *what* we are taught is not as important as the *method* by which we are taught. We may forget algebra and second-year Latin, but we remember how to obey orders, suppress our own experience, and think like everyone else. One of his descriptions of the victims of this system sounded very like the 102 class I was struggling with: "They've got that slave mentality: obliging and ingratiating on the surface but hostile and resistant underneath" (93).

Depressing, for our students are not Farber's students. Our students have been dosed with progressive education since preschool. By the third day of class, my students put their chairs in a circle, like well-modified rats, as dutifully as students in 1967 faced the front.

But before considering the unnerving consequences of this data, I wanted to retrieve another famous and widely mimeographed cultural artifact of the (so called) Revolution, which I thought would bring the discussion into clearer perspective.

This was a piece by Henry Ottinger in the *New York Times* for July 22, 1971, titled "In Short, Why Did the Class Fail?" Ottinger was then an instructor in English and a doctoral candidate at the University of Missouri. His essay proported to be a final lecture delivered at the end of his freshman composition class. He began by reviewing for the students that "I began the semester in a way that departed from the manner in which I had taught composition classes in the past. Much of my attitude at that time was influenced by Farber's book, *The Student as Nigger* [it had become a book by then] . . .

"I suggested that we try to break the mold," he continued, "that we could write papers on any subject we wanted, that we could spend class time discussing things, either 'the burning issues of the day' or otherwise." But, though students seemed to agree with his approach, "things went from initial ecstasy to final catastrophe." Students, he says, "forced" him back into assigning topics and, all in all, he concludes "this semester has been the worst I ever taught."

What followed in Ottinger's address to his students was a long coda on the phrase, "Exterminate the brutes." He accused the students of being "the most silent, reticent, paranoid bunch of people [he has] ever encountered in a group." He says he has learned that "working together (for peace or a grade) is . . . bull." "You had an opportunity to exchange ideas . . . and you were too embarrassed to do so," he says. "You had an opportunity to find out something about yourselves. . . . And as far as I can see you found out very little. You had an opportunity to explore ideas on your own and failed. Most of the papers hashed over the usual cliché-ridden topics." Finally, he says, "you had the opportunity to be free . . . and you succeeded in proving to me that freedom is slavery . . ." (33).

My children would say this sounds like me when I lose control in the kitchen at five p.m. Indeed, fashions in child-rearing and classroom management tend to run their course together. Let Mr. Rogers, let Ken Macrorie purr on; it is the tendency of things to always turn into their opposites, to fall apart and recombine. (I suppose that's why "liberation pedagogies" are now under deconstruction.) The natural work of young people is to subvert and challenge the authority of teacher and parent, no matter how "enlightened." This is perhaps their primary learning experience. They are, in some strategic sense, the opposition. Modern parents, for example, often assume, as I did, that if they set reasonable and flexible guidelines, their children will not rebel. This is rarely true, and when it is true—as when the young person is too fearful or shamefast or overly responsible to rebel—the situation is not a healthy one. Children inevitably stretch their toes over whatever line the parents have chosen to mark the edge of civilization. Perhaps some biological mechanism kicks in at puberty to make young people obnoxious so that parents can bear to give them up when the time comes. In sum, you can sit in a magic circle with your students, but you'd better look out for who's throwing the spell. "You forced me . . ." says Ottinger. This is a sorcerer's apprentice who has lost control of the charm.

Ottinger did some justice to the possibility that cultural conditioning—as much as laziness and depravity—had anesthetized his students, but I think he underrated its importance. "Rats and dogs," he says, "are conditioned, and are usually incapable of breaking that conditioning. Human beings can break conditioning if it's to their advantage," he says, but I wonder. One of the teacher's hardest jobs is to break conditioning. You can't just open the cages, as do some of my friends in the animal liberation movement, and hope the poor beasts will run free. They will cower on their familiar newspaper, by their dish of Kibbles and Bits. Set free in the wide world they will desperately try to run mazes.

As I prepared my conference paper, I didn't want to enter into a point-by-point critique of Professor Ottinger's essay, because, frankly, I sympathized with him. I understand the punitive urge that comes when one has tried one's best to create the peaceable classroom and students are *still* indulging in what Farber called passive "Uncle Tom" behavior. Few people, in my experience, become aggressive as fast as pacifists whose strategies have failed. Military people and police have more training at impulse control.

I began with a question about what turns a young idealist into an old cynic. *Students,* of course, is the obvious answer. And stress. There are some interesting studies on the relationship between stress and cynicism; but is there any way we can interrupt this hardening process and keep ourselves alive in the classroom?

I suppose that is one of the questions that has brought me to write this book, and my answers remain tentative. Back then, I settled for the preliminary insight that nothing works perfectly with students. They aren't always ready to "center," nor are we. When I taught Genna and Greg, and when I faced my first college classes, I was pretty ignorant about what was going on inside students. I think most of us were, even those who had been teaching a long time. From the mute, inglorious essays we got, what could we know of humankind? In those days I thought my students' major problems had to do with poor high school preparation or being overtired from Allis Chalmers. Even though I had a few Vietnam vets in my class, I didn't know what that meant. But now we know more about our students' inner worlds—in part because, thanks to the work of Macrorie, Elbow, Spellmeyer, and Rose—we are not reading such empty, voiceless essays.

In any class of twenty people, by a conservative law of averages, two have been sexually abused, two are struggling with their sexual identities, and two have serious problems with substance abuse. If you're lucky, it's the same two. One of my colleagues likes to remind me that eighteen-year-olds routinely test out as psychotic on the MMPI.

Then there is the teacher, desperately trying to shed his or her authoritarian conditioning. In any department of twenty, two are . . . but let's not go into it. The point is that you can't just put your chairs in a circle and forget about the human condition.

We are still getting stuck, I concluded then, in some old-fashioned (though philosophically respectable) places, trying to figure out, for example, the relationship between power and love. When I was a young teacher, I used to think the student-centered classroom was predicated on diffusion of power. As a pacifist, I was eager to give it away. I found this to be dangerous and confusing to students. Whether we like it or not as teachers, we have inherited our fathers' light saber, and we have to learn how to use it. The worst thing we can do is pretend we don't have power.

On the other hand, Jerry Farber said something in his essay I found disquieting at the time: that teachers should learn to thrive on love and admiration rather than on fear and respect. In fact, I responded, nothing messes up my classroom faster than love. The problem is related to power. As Harvey Cox says, You can't be I / Thou with a whole city, and if you try to be, some dangerous unreality is in play.

I keep using the word *dangerous*. Well, we're in the heart of darkness here. As I wrote my conference paper, I couldn't resist working toward "The horror!" by way of conclusion, though I would have preferred to be more upbeat. This was as optimistic as I could be: if we are stuck on issues of love and power, no wonder we are confused. What else is there? I'm happy to be in a profession that deals with life's basic concerns. The question may not be has the new pedagogy changed students, but has it changed us? On my good days I think that teaching is some kind of spiritual journey: what *we* learn is more important than what *they* learn, just as what Marlow learns is more important than what Kurtz learns. What he learns gives Marlow the right to sit crosslegged on the deck of a ship telling stories to business majors. On my bad days, I think, there you have it: "the horror!"

The Difficulties of the Examined Life

That's what I had to say at the conference in 1986, and that's pretty much how I wrote it up in an essay for *College English*. It disturbed people who preferred my earlier visions of lambs lying down with lions, but really I was just trying to get more deeply into the reality of life in that zoo or jungle. And even at that, I hadn't begun to articulate the depth of despair I was feeling, despair so keen that I almost left the profession—though the difficulties of teaching are, I guess, simply the difficulties of any examined life. When I was young I was prepared to face, even exuberantly, the problems that lay ahead. I remember writing something down in my commonplace book about "courting doubt and despair as the price of knowing." But doubt is a mudslide, an oil slick, a spirit of dark water as the Irish say. It drains the exuberance. Every couple of semesters Doubt comes to visit me with the message that I have spent my life on a foolish quest, that perhaps I should take up nursing or, say, folk art—like the man in Wisconsin who built a miniature world out of cement and old bottle glass, or the one who strung his house in thousands of chiming beer cans, or the one who planted deer antlers everywhere instead of flowers—that I should leave something palpable behind.

But I stay in teaching because all the models we have for spiritual process—religious, mythic, what have you—tell us that it doesn't matter whether we are right or wrong or successful but merely that we remain faithful to a vision. And that when it's easy, it isn't worth much. Let me repeat and rephrase: because teaching is some kind of spiritual inquiry, what *we* learn is more important than what *they* learn. It is more important, at least, to *our* passage; they are going someplace else; they are in a different myth. Maybe they are in a TV sitcom. This isn't to say that I don't care about what students learn; of course I do. But we cannot control their reactions, we can only determine our own inner weather.

I feel compelled to belabor this idea because recently a serious young graduate student congratulated me for writing parody. He thought that my attempt to define a spirituality of teaching represented some kind of clever deconstruction of our fundamental illusions. No, I'm not kidding about the idea of spiritual inquiry. I'm from the prairie where we have a deficient sense of irony. I'm just blathering in all sincerity, like Keats, though less eloquently, about soulmaking.

But I don't fault this young graduate student for his cynicism: I was the one who had snickered at Ihab Hassan.

It's risky to talk about the spirituality of teaching, though it's becoming fashionable. "Spirituality," these days, can mean anything you want it to mean, and for that reason I am tempted to discard it forever from my box of words. But instead I'll try to be precisely clear about my own intent. First, I'm not looking for a back door into church. My relationship to organized religion has been rather like Groucho Marx's to country clubs: I wouldn't join one that would be demented enough to have me as a member. But I am using the word "spirituality" in a rather strict sense: as "of, or having to do with the central religious traditions of humankind." I want to be precise here because I think that amorphous spiritualities can be easily co-opted to serve the purposes of fascism and totalitarianism. Hitler was a great manipulator of "spirituality." The religious traditions that nurture me—and from which I have liberally quoted in this book—are Roman Catholic, Zen Buddhist, and Quaker. Dogma is not relevant to my present purposes. What is relevant is discipline: a way of being-in-time that these traditions propose. Tad Dunne, in his book on the Jesuit philosopher Bernard Lonergan, has made this point, to my mind, very well:

> The self-loss which mystics praise and all great world religions preach must now be understood as a strategy for revolution. It is the loss of concern and fear for one's reputation while one is engaged in dialog, disagreement, and debate. Indeed, all the old spiritual doctrines about mortification, self-effacement, and abandonment to the will of God can now be understood empirically. We no longer have to accept them as mysterious practices that will make us better persons. We can now understand how they make us better—because we put being attentive above being smug, being intelligent above being narrow-minded, being reasonable above being a dreamer, being responsible above being hedonistic, and being in love above being stiff-necked and hard of heart. The authenticity that results from obedience to the transcendental precepts . . . changes ourselves and our world for the better in intelligible and verifiable ways (190).

There was a time when it seemed important to understand social-epistemic discourse and what the heck the word *heuristic* meant. Now it seems important to understand abandonment and self-effacement. When I began thinking about the peaceable classroom, I conceived it as a *goal;* now I see it as, in the Zen sense, a *practice.* At a Zen sitting, one doesn't (theoretically) worry about whether it goes well or badly, one simply tries to "practice." In daily life, one attempts to cultivate a similar attitude of nonjudgmental presence. I'll say more about this later, but, since I've introduced the subject of stress, I'll add that such an attitude, on the rare occasions I can bring it to bear, helps me to get through the teaching day with more grace than was available to me in my exterminator days.

Just as an example, let's look at one of the most difficult aspects of our job: reading student papers, which is a burden we have to come to terms with sooner or later or quit teaching. And we come to terms in ways that seem to replicate our own undergraduate experience. Some of my colleagues pull all-nighters, grading a hundred or so essays into the winter dawn. Others mark them in front of the TV—that being, as one of my friends says, "where they were conceived."

When I started to look at grading papers as an aspect of spiritual practice, one of the first things I noticed was how much unacknowledged physical tension I was bringing to the task. My body, if I bothered to scan it, was full of nervous clutching. I seemed to be in a "fight or flight" stance. Maintaining a critical attitude has consequences for the nervous system. They may not necessarily be bad consequences; we all know people who seem to need hostility to keep the blood circulating. But I was able to determine that the results were not good for me. What I am now trying to cultivate—and with by no means perfect success—is an attitude of *friendly visiting* as though the student were present with all her life and concerns spread out, as though I had nothing else in the world to do than to talk with her. I think I spend more time commenting on papers now, but I leave the process much less exhausted. I do not dread it. It takes energy to dread things, energy for which there are better uses.

The Vietnamese Buddhist Thích Nh'ât Hanh in his commentary on the Sutra of Mindfulness calls this attitude of calm attention "washing dishes to wash dishes." I have his words pinned up over my kitchen sink, but they would be equally appropriate over my desk:

> If while washing dishes, we think only of the cup of tea that awaits us, thus hurrying to get the dishes out of the way as if they were a nuisance, then we are not "washing dishes to wash dishes." What's more, we are not alive during the time we are washing the dishes. In fact we are completely incapable of realizing the miracle of life while standing at the sink. If we can't wash the dishes, the chances are we won't be able to drink our tea either. While drinking the cup of tea, we will only be thinking of other things. Thus we are sucked away into the future—and we are incapable of actually living one minute of life (4-5).

This may strike the reader as a peculiar approach. My children, on the rare occasions when they stand at the kitchen sink, have declined to adopt mindfulness as a spiritual perspective. They refuse to do dishes without simultaneous access to radio, TV, and telephone—as, not infrequently, do I. When I act mindfully, though, I get more done, which is useful if there's more at stake than the dishes. Mindfulness—if this alone recommends it to the Western mind—is efficient.

Jerry Farber wrote a thoughtful reply to my *College English* article (*CE*, Vol. 52, No. 2, February, 1990). He stuck to his point about love, for which I'm grateful, because it made me think more deeply about my own inhibitions. Women, I'm afraid, can't be too soft in this business. My women friends and I, as we struggled simultaneously to keep our chairs in a circle, get tenure, and maintain some kind of professional credibility, used to talk about this problem all the time: will our teaching style be perceived as feminine, motherly? In those days of pantyhose and banker suits, "So what?" did not seem an appropriate response, though now it's the one I'd give. Farber also draws our attention to the problem of how those of us who persisted in a radical critique of the educational system had to invent a body of technique to replace the old one (135). What were we to invent it out of? I'm inventing mine out of poetry and the principles of nonviolence. Ultimately, though, I have to say that those principles reflect a tradition of values. Once again, this is not an apology, but an attempt to fairly disclose the premises of the argument.

Four

The Force that Through the Green Fuse Drives the Flower

In the last few chapters, I've been trying to view composition theory through the lens of a nonviolent discipline, responding simply to an understanding shaped by my reading of war literature. In the next few chapters, I'd like to reweave another set of insights from those texts and talk about them in terms of our teaching life. I repeat Ihab Hassan's question: Can we teach English so that people stop killing each other? And I would like to center the discussion in an understanding of the English classroom as a place to foster the inner world. I follow here Václav Havel's insight that a certain kind of contemplative life is synonymous with responsible behavior in a community. These are the qualities Havel believes the politician of the future should cultivate, and if the politician, why not the citizen?

> Soul, individual spirituality, first-hand personal insight into things; the courage to be himself and go the way his conscience points, humility in the face of the mysterious order of Being, confidence in its own natural direction, and above all, trust in his own subjectivity as his principal link with the subjectivity of the world (15).

On this path of soul making, I hope, we left our freshman writer; let us now see how literary study can contribute to fostering Havel's ideal of citizenship in a new world community.

One day, about twenty years ago, I went into my classroom to teach English in a room where someone else had been teaching English the hour before. This diagram was on the blackboard:

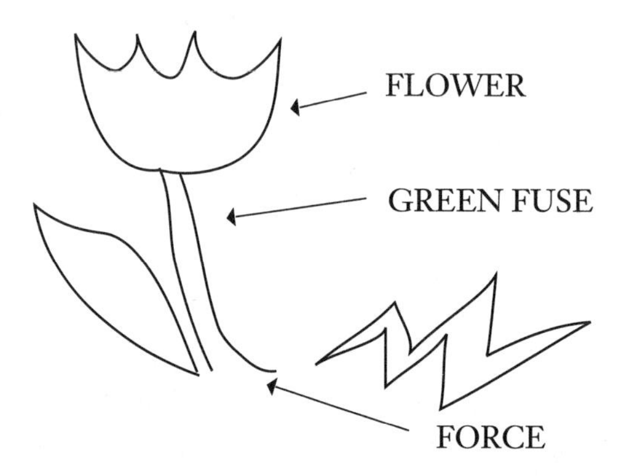

I stared at it awhile. It was worth pondering.

For anyone not familiar with Dylan Thomas's poetry, let me explain that the teacher before me had no doubt been attempting to explicate:

The force that through the green fuse drives the flower
Drives my green age; that blasts the roots of trees
Is my destroyer . . . (8)

Our classroom was one of those abominations built in the late fifties—white cement walls, no windows—the world's biggest urinal, one of my colleagues called it. What could we know of green fuses in that "plain without a feature, bare and brown"? WE do the blasting now, WE light the fuses.

In the course on war literature discussed earlier, one of the central themes we discovered was a progressive alienation of humankind from nature. To the gun-man, nature closes her green doors; the pastoral is repeatedly violated by falling planes, wandering lunatics, and decomposing corpses. War literature warns not only of the literal destruction of the ecosystem but of the violation of those aspects of human consciousness that "nature" as literary subject tends to externalize: spirit, contemplation, the anima.

And though the last lights off the black West went
Oh, morning, at the brown brink eastward, springs—
Because the Holy Ghost over the bent
World broods . . .

writes Gerard Manley Hopkins (66), in a phrase that has ironic reverberations in the nuclear age. Hopkins's "freshness deep down things" has remarkable vitality—though one wonders how long it can resist our chemical dumping—and the least touch of nature has an appeal to consciousness out of all proportion to a limited encounter. I once taught a gifted young writer who lived in the Milwaukee inner city. He wrote as precisely and enchantedly about grass and bugs as does Annie Dillard. "How do you know these things?" I asked him one day. "Oh, there was a freeway overpass near my house, with this little patch of grass . . . I would lie there day after day. . . ."

In Minnesota, our students are likely to feel at home in the woods where great numbers go to kill animals for sport. I'm not a hunter, and I don't like students to skip class, but I never mind the empty desks that greet us on those sacred northern holidays that mark the openings of each hunting season. Hunting season yields many good essays; rarely are they about killing, and when they are, they are often about the discovery of disgust with it all. Spending a few days in the woods with one's father seems to me more important at critical points in the semester than sitting in front of me on a molded plastic chair. Call it research on Dylan Thomas.

Whatever spiritual sites our students visit are worthy of respect, though their choices might differ from ours. Schooling used to be a monastic occupation: is it possible for our modern classrooms to retrieve these origins? Teachers of literature and writing are uniquely situated to mediate this question. The inner world is what literature is all about. Why have we forgotten that?

Probably because in the last hundred years "thinking" has come to mean, more and more exclusively, scientific thinking. Truth has come to equal scientific verifiability. To earn a doctorate in literature has seemed, from this worldly perspective, not quite tough-minded—soft, while physics is hard. As a result, our field has become more and more dominated by theory, jargon, and critical paraphernalia in an attempt to disguise its claim on the mere unverifiable heart. It's easier nowadays for the intelligent lay person to read *King Lear* than to read the average journal of Shakespeare studies—if that person has not been put off Lear altogether by an undergraduate diet of post-structuralism. We're told that the decline in English majors has something to do with the job market for liberal arts graduates, which I think is only partly true. Mostly it has to do with the decline of attention to literature—what the students, after all, come for. They ask us for bread and we give them Saussurean linguistics.

A plain without a feature, bare and brown,
No blade of grass, no sign of neighborhood,
Nothing to eat and nowhere to sit down.

—W.H. Auden, "The Shield of Achilles"
(454)

Tears for Things

It's the first day back after a long vacation and I have an 8:15 freshman class. When I was a young teacher, my older colleagues would advise me under such conditions to, "Start with a bang. Remind them that there are only two weeks 'til exams." Or if you are too catatonic yourself, "Give a pop quiz."

A lot of the advice we are given as young teachers runs counter not only to the often-introverted professorial temperament, but to the deepest wellsprings of our discipline.

If you are not fond of pops and bangs, you may prefer to approach such mornings more softly. Every group of people has its field of relationships in place before the interloping teacher comes on the scene; it is possible, and perhaps wise, to enter it as a dancer or gentle guest rather than in the spirit of disruption. (Many of my colleagues manage to get to class before the first student, but I have never been organized enough to be so gracious.) On this particular morning, I read for a while from the work of the Tibetan Buddhist Chögyam Trungpa: "We must continue in the face of tremendous opposition. No one is encouraging us to open, and still we must peel away the layers of the heart . . ." (Goldberg, 12).

We write for twenty minutes about anything that may be on our minds; then we share reflections in small groups. It is particularly important to do this today because we have been touched by loss. One of the freshmen, after a night of bar-hopping, was killed in a car accident on his way back to the university.

Does this sadly common kind of incident have anything to do with an English class?

I once complimented a woman I know, a recovering alcoholic and chemical dependency counselor, on the daily beauty of her dress and grooming. "I'm in an attraction program," she replied. "I'm advertising a conscious life." So are we, I hope. We are living—with style, if possible—the discipline of speaking from the heart. It's discipline and it's hard (Buddhists will remember that Trungpa had his problems): a monastic exercise, a divine office; it is zazen, Zen sitting; it is a kind of yoga, this peeling away the layers of the heart. Modern life contrives to shut up, or shut down, the spirit. Offices and shopping malls, diners and even slick modern churches are not made for crying and laughing and love. The need to speak remains intense, warring against the repressions of culture. The need to feel remains intense until the capacity to feel becomes dull and atrophied.

O may my heart's truth
Still be sung
On this high hill in a year's turning

writes Dylan Thomas (97). I think it would be OK for English class, every once in awhile, to sing the heart's truth.

As I wander among the small groups reading to each other, I see that many people are crying.

Odysseus says he wants to go back to Ithaca because it's a place "where there are tears for things."

That would be another good definition of the peaceable classroom.

Compassion as a Mode of Inquiry: The Case of John Woolman

For the last few years, I've taught a course called *Texts and Traditions*, which traces the origins of modern thought from ancient Greece to the present. Rationalism, in the general sense, has been the dominant strain in our tradition, and that is, on the whole, a good thing. I've never been persuaded by certain anthropological fantasies about happy ancestors sitting around the camp fire playing cooperative games. I suspect those ancient people were ghost-ridden, demon-ridden, and that by and large a good dose of rationality would have helped them to get their caves in order. But at about the time of Descartes, most of us would now agree, the rational agenda whirled out of balance. We would agree—to the extent we do, if I have not begged an important question here—largely because of the persuasive analyses of such feminist writers as Nel Noddings and Carol Gilligan, who have tried to retrieve our sense of multiple ways of knowing.

It is in this spirit that I suggest we look at *compassion as a mode of critical inquiry.* I believe it is possible to examine our subject matter, whatever it may be, through a glass of tenderness as well as through the glass of reason. I will not put this idea, for the moment, into a feminist context, because I did not originally discover it there; I found it in the writings of Blaise Pascal and John Woolman. They will help me, I hope, to state more conscientiously what I mean by "the heart," which I have referred to earlier with such careless abandon.

Pascal, no great friend of Descartes, was the first modern philosopher (that I am aware of) to talk about *le coeur* as a way of knowing rather than as a sentimental faculty. A master mathematician who laid the foundation of infinitesimal and integral calculus, Pascal yet mistrusted the intrusion of reason into areas that reason could not adequately interrogate. We may repeat, by way of explaining odd romances, Pascal's famous maxim: "The heart has its reasons which reason knows not of." But perhaps we do not inquire too precisely into what he meant. He was trying, I think, to protect some space for an epistemology that does not depend upon the rational intellect as its solitary champion.

The heart, in Pascal's sense, is a metaphoric site, but so is reason. We do not know where consciousness exists—in the head, in the solar plexus, or in a field around the body—nor can we cleanly separate out and anatomize the operations of feeling and thinking. Mechanistic physiology has, however, so relentlessly pressed on our attention the idea of the brain as a kind of computer that we may *think* we know the mind in the same way that we know the pancreas. We do not. If we sit attentively at birth or death, we will quickly discover the inadequacy of our models of consciousness. In the same way, we can sit attentively with literary texts.

After spending a few seasons with Pascal, I happened to return again to John Woolman's *Journal*, and I was struck by how this eighteenth-century pacifist—a provincial, middle-class Quaker who was far from the intellectual currents of his day—took for granted that thought and feeling are one. He seemed to have been passed over by the Dissociation of Sensibility so troubling to the descendents of Donne and Lord Herbert of Cherbury.

Woolman's autobiography opens with the sort of "expressive" writing that some modern composition theorists regard with suspicion. He recalls how, as a boy of twelve, he committed an act that challenged his sense of who he was:

> . . . once, going to a neighbor's house, I saw on the way a robin sitting on her nest; and as I came near she went off, but having

> young ones, flew about and with many cries expressed her concern for them. I stood and threw stones at her, till one striking her, she fell down dead. At first I was pleased with the exploit, but after a few minutes was seized with horror, as having in a sportive way killed an innocent creature while she was careful for her young (in *Quaker Spirituality*, 163).

As my students sometimes do in the aftermath of hunting season, Woolman goes on to meditate on the innate principle of kindness he senses within himself: if we listen to it, we become "tender hearted and sympathizing." If we do not, the sympathetic faculty will shut down from disuse: ". . . being frequently and totally rejected, the mind shuts itself up in a contrary disposition" (164).

As his spiritual journey continues, Woolman learns to try the moral world before the tribunal of sympathy. We might say he takes the cultural scales from his eyes or that he puts on the glasses of tenderness. Either way, the empirical world comes to look different to him than it looks to most everyone else. Slavery does not seem acceptable, nor, later, does the violation of Native American rights. He anticipates, in fact, most of the liberation issues of our time, including animal welfare:

> . . . I believe where . . . the true spirit of government [is] watchfully attended to, a tenderness toward all creatures made subject to us will be experienced, and a care felt in us that we do not lessen that sweetness of life in the animal creation which the great Creator intends for them under our government (228).

For Woolman, in contrast to most men after Descartes, reason was not the most apt and appropriate instrument for problem-solving; sympathy was. The vision sympathy gave him, in turn, became a stimulus to challenge the moral boundaries of his class and culture. Even within the Religious Society of Friends, rational arguments had kept oppressive social arrangements in place. And Woolman was capable of creating subtle counterarguments (he was not "irrational"), but the arguments followed, they did not precede, the motion of the heart.

Looking at texts like Woolman's and trying to lay aside for the moment our Enlightenment model of how the mind works—looking merely at such texts as though one were newly arrived from another galaxy and did not know anything about how consciousness operates on the planet Earth—I doubt we would hypothesize anything like the traditional Western epistemological model. We would not from these data come up with an image of busy Reason directing the orchestra of Perception. Perhaps we alien observers would say, "For these creatures, social change seems to follow from a motion of—what shall we call it?—*le coeur*, as one of their philosophers has written." Walter Brueggemann, writing on the nature of prophecy, has put it this way: "Compassion constitutes a radical form of criticism, for it announces that the hurt is to be taken seriously, that the hurt is not to be accepted as normal and natural but is an abnormal and unacceptable condition for humanness" (85).

As I examine the case of John Woolman, it illuminates for me our professional debate between "expressivist" rhetorics, often critiqued as individualistic and self-centered, and "social-epistemic" theory that, at a presumed cost to individual autonomy, aims for social transformation. In Woolman—as in Thoreau, Shelley, or Blake—we see that the individual vision and the impulse to social reform always double back on each other. Personal voice—prophecy, in Brueggemann's sense—disrupts the state of communal numbness in which most of us exist. "Empires live by numbness," Walter Brueggemann goes on to say. "Empires, in their militarism, expect numbness about the human cost of war. Corporate economies expect blindness to the cost in terms of poverty and exploitation. Governments and societies of domination go to great lengths to keep the numbness intact" (85–86). Prophecy, he says, interrupts our sense of business-as-usual by uncovering hidden darkness, by a true naming of what we prefer to euphemize. "Thus, compassion that might be seen simply as generous goodwill is in fact criticism of the system, forces, and ideologies that produce the hurt" (86).

I defend personal writing, then, because I think that some form of self-interrogation is essential to the formation of *le coeur:* personal subjectivity, as Havel puts it, becoming the principal link with the subjectivity of the world. Besides, as I have said earlier, it allows each of us to try our unique experience against the univocal cultural story Western man has made up about the nature of reality. A work of literature—especially considered from the point of view of someone marginal to the canonical discussion, or written by such an outsider—can tell us that the hurt is to be taken seriously; so can a piece of student writing tell us that.

Woolman's interiority was nurtured by a Quaker community of search—one that significantly valued the feminine—as well as by a recollected family and a habit of silence and self-examination.

Our students may have, by contrast, only an English class to nurture their inner life, their prophetic spirits.

Conform, Go Crazy, or Become an Artist

The title of this piece is inscribed on the T-shirt I'm wearing as I write.

I don't wear this shirt very often because it seems to make people angry, and as a pacifist, that's not the effect I want to have. Besides, it takes energy to get up every morning and decide what ideology you're going to espouse that day. My subject of the moment, however, will be *why* this shirt makes people mad, so I'll stop and give you a few moments to examine your own subjective reactions.

Take a minute right now. Freewrite if you want to.

In St. Paul, Minnesota, we're just a little wary of artists. On the prairie, we mistrust anybody who doesn't conform. Such a person might be off dreaming when the cows get loose.

Are you still freewriting? If you like what you're writing, keep on. Don't pay any attention to me. You've already figured it out.

Here is my question: What would it be like to teach from the conviction that our students are artists, poets, indeed, from the knowledge that we ourselves are poets? How would that change the classroom? Previously I have situated my philosophy within spiritual tradition; now, with a slight shift, I will try to locate it in the house of art. Like William Blake, with whom I have otherwise nothing useful in common, I find it difficult to separate religion from art.

I want to begin by talking about our grief.

Most of us who teach English were probably once writers. I think we feel a lot of unacknowledged sadness because graduate school and five-course loads and the tenure process and writing-in-red all over our students' papers and, above all, the atmosphere of criticism that poisons the air of our universities, grade schools, alternative schools, Montessori, and home schools has taken our art and our voices. There was a long period in my professional life when I read no poetry because the pain of having given up my own work and spirit was too intense. When I joined the Twin Cities Area Writing Project in 1982, I fought the freewriting process because (and this is a revision of my earlier account) at some level I knew that awakening words again would hurt like blood flowing back to a deadened limb. I thought the pain might lead me to option two: go crazy.

When you look around in the University—but this is equally true of any modern institution—if you let a number of things enter your field of vision, you would probably have to resign in a righteous huff. We are a little like the Germans who lived around Auschwitz in 1942. Those people knew where the rail lines led, but if they had truly let it enter their consciousness they would have had to go crazy. I have another T-shirt that says, "Denial, It's Not a River in Egypt," but I'll wear that to write a different book.

These days, our rail lines (or superhighways) lead to the megamalls, to enslavement in the culture of trade and commerce, to the alienation which perhaps no one has described as well as Karl Marx: "It has drowned the most heavenly ecstasies of religious fervor, of chivalrous enthusiasm, and [even] of philistine sentimentalism, in the icy water of egotistical calculation. It has resolved personal worth into exchange value . . ." (18). Lewis Hyde, in his perceptive book, *The Gift*, has made a similar analysis:

> After the Reformation the empires of commodity expanded without limit until soon all things—from land and labor to erotic life, religion and culture—were bought and sold like shoes. It is now the age of the practical and self-made man, who, like the private eye of the movies, survives in the world by adopting the detached style of the alien; he lives in the spirit of usury, which is the spirit of boundaries and divisions (139).

Interestingly enough, in terms of our previous discussion, Hyde describes this usurious life as a "hardening of the heart," which he contrasts to the "expanding heart" of the Middle Ages, where "deviance" was, by definition, a failure of generosity.

Most academic activities today serve, I fear, the purposes of capitalism and not the economy of gift, of art.

But let me explain a little more about what I think it means to be an artist, and why I think art constitutes an affront to a culture worth affronting. When I wear this shirt in Minnesota, people give me a look that seems to say "Who Do You Think You Are?" Or they argue with me. Are those really the options?—Conform, Go Crazy, or Be an Artist? They don't want to believe it. They want to propose a more logical division of the question: lots of artists are crazy, most artists conform. But it's all a variation on "Who Do You Think You Are?"

I think they have a notion that artists are an elite cadre of people who lounge around making smart remarks and sneering at people who work for a living. If that's your notion, I need to take a moment to refine my vision.

Many Buddhist traditions cherish the idea that certain holy ones may choose not to become enlightened but return to the wheel of illusion again and again until all humankind is enlightened. If I could hold up an ideal for us as teachers, as poets, it would be that. One artist friend of mine scrupulously calls herself a "painter." She says it is up to others to call her an "artist." I sympathize with that approach. I don't want anybody to call me a poet until all earth's children are poets. Let's all be poets. Let's make this so much a part of our self-definition that nobody stands out, nobody has to be asked, "Who Do You Think You Are?"

Are you still freewriting? If you're not, here's a question to get you started: What do you do for ecstasy?

That's a question we can't ask ourselves often enough. Art, in the sense I mean, does not necessarily require a pen or paint brush, but it requires us to stand outside our ego boundaries. In "A Dialogue of Self and Soul," W. B. Yeats writes, "We must laugh and we must sing, / We are blest by everything, / Everything we look upon is blest" (232). Let's put that on a sweatshirt and wear it to next year's professional conferences.

Recently I've been reading in a minor genre we might call "Homage to Dead English Teachers." These pieces usually appear in alumni magazines; the title of one I read recently says it best: "He Only Wrote in Red." This professor, according to the article, spent his whole life writing careful comments on student papers when he might have had it in him to be a *real* writer. It's so sad, so touching, such a sacrifice say the alumni magazines.

But is it? I want to know what we are giving our lives *for*? Who is writing these tributes to the Dead Professors' Society? Sharon Olds? Toni Morrison? Don't count on it. I once had a very instructive conversation with an alum who started on one of those maudlin poor-old-professor tales, "He would go over my stories, write essays in the margin, never getting to his own work. . . ." And who was my interlocutor, the recipient of such professorial philanthropy? He was a man who ran a company under indictment for dumping toxic waste in the Mississippi River. It's not my business to judge him, but it's my business to decide what's worth *my* life.

Of course, artists are such selfish pigs. That's one reason why this shirt makes people mad in Minnesota. But really, I think that if you have a big splash of ecstasy in your life every day you are going to teach students something finer than *buy low, sell high*. Maybe you'll teach them, not by what you say but by who you are, to live their lives as a standing affront to the ravaging mercantile mentality. Teach them to give their lives away mindfully rather than mindlessly, with generosity rather than with calculation.

By and large, in the academy, we worship the god of commerce, whose religion is antithetical to art. But there is another god we worship who also kills our poems. She dances on our art like Kali with her necklace of skulls. She is the god of criticism.

It's important to examine every once in a while the deep structures of our professional lives. What is college teaching really about? My dad was a buyer in a department store, which is probably why I hate commerce so much. He got into that line of work because he liked color and design and doing window displays; but, one day, too deeply committed to ever turn back, he said to me, "This job is all about making people buy things they don't need. And every day our goal is to sell more than we sold that same day the year before, world without end. Amen." After he thought about that awhile, my dad got sick and died.

I had a similar awakening about the deep structures of *our* profession a few years ago while I was on sabbatical living in a Quaker community devoted (however imperfectly) to affirming and developing every member's gifts. In this atmosphere my spirit expanded dangerously, and I remembered that that's what teaching *should* be about but isn't: discerning the gift. Too often, by contrast, the central activity of our discipline is judging. The major thing we have learned to do in life is to assign grades—to essays, to colleagues up for tenure, to ideas, to new books, to the latest play or restaurant. (Recently my young daughter had the honor of meeting a restaurant critic. She had never encountered such a person, never imagined such a life. "Why should I care what somebody else thinks of my food?" she asked me. "I only care what *I* think of my food.")

Now, it's not my intent to shred critical conventions from Aristotle to the present. It would be a terrible thing not to have standards. How would we know what we like? How would we know where we stand in the pecking order? But criticism has rather lately become the *central* shaping principal of our discipline. In most graduate schools, it's more important to read critics than to read poets, as we all know. This is especially weird when you consider that criticism as a predictor of artistic staying power is about as reliable as the psychic forecasts printed each New Year's Day. Criticism misplaced John Donne for 300 years. Nobody understood Emily Dickinson in her own time. Edgar Guest, now *there* was a poet.

Our obsession with judgment may be a unique legacy of our Puritan heritage. We are all trying to be "saved" by being incorrigibly perfect teachers, parents, liberals, vegetarians, or whatever. To be perfect, you need standards. You need to know where the sheep and goats are respectively penned. The scriptural roots of this Puritan concept are dubious, however, for the Greek word *teleios*, which the King James Bible translates as "perfect," means something closer to "whole," which, if we think about it, is also what "perfect" meant to the Jacobean reader. Be whole. It's a classical concept celebrated by Aristotle in the *Nichomachean Ethics*, his ideal of the fully integrated human being. In asking us to think about being integrated, teleological, and whole (rather than faultless), I am not suggesting we give up our habit of critical thinking and wander around in a haze of phony good feeling. I hate that. Critical thinking has traditionally involved stating the merits of something, stating its weaknesses, contextualizing it in a tradition, and comparing it to others of its kind—all necessary operations of culture. But what I'd like to see is more balance. Mostly we are taught and encouraged to find fault. In academic culture, the one who is most negative is often considered the most intellectual. What's going on here? We are rewarding sick, perverse, poisonous behavior. We should stop promoting these people and simply set them to making commercials for breakfast cereals.

Criticism is necessary to the intellectual enterprise, but there should be some sort of just war theory devised to govern its excesses. We should at least remind ourselves that we are engaged in an activity that has more potential for pain than benefit; such an attitude might keep us from taking it all too seriously. When I am in my critiquing mind, I am not as tranquil as when I am in my pondering mind. My claws are at the veins of life. When I am comparing, I am not contemplating essential beauty. I feel myself to be a happier, gentler, and healthier human when I am in poet-mind—receptive, unjudging, listening—than when I am in critic-mind.

As Marcus Aurelius says over and over, the only world we have is the world of our own mind, dyed by our thoughts and habits of judging. Selfish pig that I am, I want to live in an artist's room. Yet, what happens in the life of an individual affects the whole. If we teach our students to be ninja critics, that pedagogy supports a certain quality of consciousness on the planet. If, by contrast, we teach them to live part time in the house of art, we create a different future.

I regularly teach a part of our freshman literature-and-composition sequence focusing on poetry. For years I had terrible luck teaching this course as it was "supposed" to be taught, namely by making students write six critical essays about poetry. On the final evaluations, students would write things like "I have unexpectedly enjoyed the poems we've read this semester, though I never intend to read any more." This year I began to use the Brown and Glass text, *Important*

Words, along with a standard poetry anthology. *Important Words* is essentially a beginner's creative writing text that leads students through simple exercises in poetry writing. One of its strange features is that it mixes up examples of student poetry with poetry by real, published, but often somewhat obscure poets. So the book forces you to take each piece on its own merits. It's very dislocating. You read something interesting or daring and you say, "Now let's see, is this by a *poet* or just some nobody?"

Critical standards. Yes, we need them. As we say about the weather in Minnesota, it keeps out the riffraff.

My experiment with mixing creative writing and the writing of critical essays was not an unqualified success, but I think it nurtured one important possibility: the chance for students to see, for one semester, through the eyes of art. And it reminded me, too, to see with those eyes.

Most of us do not get enough opportunity to explore that way of knowing, though we have a few programs to bring artists and poets into the schools. At the college level, of course, we have that odd hybrid, the creative writing course, which usually has to be taught by someone with a Ph.D. Why? Well, probably, because if the poet doesn't have a Ph.D., the other members of the department will one way or another peck him to death. But every time we send a poet through a Ph.D. program we are likely to do considerable damage to art. How do I know this? Last February I took a workshop with lots of creative writing teachers and poets-in-the-schools and here are two things that happened:

One poet-professor when asked what problems she had with her writing, commented that because she was a college teacher she had no emotional life, that she spent her days in a flat and loveless institutional environment uncongenial to the inner world. Her comment won lots of acclaim in the group. Almost everybody agreed. Pathetic. And a tragic capitulation.

Second thing. The workshop leader, who was the poet Galway Kinnell, asked the group to write on the topic of "something you have never tried to put into words." Then he went around the circle and asked people to read. I'm sure you're familiar with this technique. We expect our students to respond to it every day. He said, as most of us say, "You can pass if you want to." Guess who passed? Everybody.

Jerry Farber used to say the profession is short on balls. Barbara Lawrence in her oft-anthologized essay, "Four-letter Words Can Hurt You," says that the word *balls* (which she demurely manages not to print) presumably "suggests little more than a mechanical shape" and recommends to our attention the more elegant "testes" which means, she reminds us, "'witnesses' (from the Latin *testis*)" (100) Well, we are short on witness, too.

Many of you are familiar with Carolyn Forché's poem, "The Colonel:"

> There was some talk then of how difficult it had become to govern. The parrot said hello on the terrace. The colonel told it to shut up, and pushed himself from the table. My friend said to me with his eyes: say nothing. The colonel returned with a sack used to bring groceries home. He spilled many human ears on the table. They were like dried peach halves. There is no other way to say this. He took one of them in his hands, shook it in our faces, dropped it into a water glass. It came alive there. I am tired of fooling around he said. As for the rights of anyone, tell your people they can go fuck themselves. He swept the ears to the floor with his arm and held the last of his wine in the air. Something for your poetry, no? he said. Some of the ears on the floor caught this scrap of his voice. Some of the ears on the floor were pressed to the ground (16).

This poem is about El Salvador. It's also about our students and about the kind of people they become, getting into their Toyotas every day, or about those who don't make it through rehab and don't get the Toyotas. And it is about us, even about the poets in the schools. The parrot is saying hello on the terrace.

Please take a little risk every day. Let's not ask our students to go it alone.

The question for me is: are we going to allow our spirits to be crushed by the terms our discipline imposes on us? The terms defined by capitalism and criticism? How can we resist?

I will answer with a recipe from Walt Whitman. I invite you to frame this selection from the 1855 preface to *Leaves of Grass* and put it over your desk. Let it guide the choices you make on a two week, all-expense-paid trial basis.

> This is what you shall do: Love the earth and sun and the animals, despise riches, give alms to everyone that asks, stand up for the stupid and crazy, devote your income and labor to others, hate tyrants, argue not concerning God, have patience and indulgence toward the people, take off your hat to nothing known or unknown or to any man or number of men, go freely with powerful uneducated persons and with the young and with the mothers of families ... re-examine all you have been told at school or church or in any book, dismiss whatever insults your own soul, and your very flesh shall be a great poem ... (11).

Peacemaking and the Antic Spirit

The economy of gift, of art, is fundamentally opposed to the economy of war. In our usurious era, the "bleeding heart," which Lewis Hyde associates with its original iconography of generous tenderness, has now become the image of "the young man of dubious mettle with an embarassing inability to limit his compassion. . . . Now the deviant is the heart that does not keep its own counsel and touches others with feeling, not reckoning" (139).

Peacemaking, conflict resolution, nonviolent discipline—call it what you may—if you find these issues discussed in school curricula at all, you'll probably find them in the political science department or the theology department. Just now, however, I'd like to look at nonviolence as an *art form* and ask how those of us whose business it is to look at art forms can contribute to the study of peace and world community.

A few summers ago, I went to a camp in Northern Minnesota sponsored by a Quaker organization called Friends for a Nonviolent World. One of our resource people was Larry Cloud Morgan, a Native American artist and activist, who had just finished a long prison term for his part in a civil disobedience action. Larry, a gentle, serious, middle-aged man of great dignity and presence, was there not to talk about nonviolent discipline but to share Ojibwa ceremonials, as a way of helping us to understand the spiritual vision of native peoples and something about our own relationship to the earth.

One night he invited us all to a solemn council fire in the tepee that happened to be on our property. It was dark. A fire was burning in the center of the circle. We took our shoes off and entered along the traditional clockwise path. A drum was beating and the sacred pipe passed from hand to hand. We were asked to hold it in silence and pray for our families.

It was a solemn occasion, there in the great centered silence of the North, and what happened to me? I got the giggles. I buried my face in my daughter's shoulder and snorted. I desperately reached backward with my bare feet, trying for some slack in the tepee that I could crawl through. But I knew I would get stuck. Thinking about getting stuck made me laugh some more, while self-possessed teenagers stared at me with contempt and my daughter tried to slide over into another family. Larry looked at me impassively in the firelight and chanted in Ojibwa. I shook with laughter and helpless shame.

The next morning I slunk in to breakfast. Friends kindly looked away. I sat as far as I could from Larry as we ate our pancakes. I kept my eyes on the blueberries, as though they might try to run for it. I felt humiliated. I thought I had hurt Larry's feelings and insulted his traditions. I drooped through lunch and dinner.

Later, when I found Larry in a corner drawing pictures, I crept over to apologize.

"Mary," he said. "I want to tell you the story of Heyoka. Heyoka is the spirit of mischief in the Ojibwa tradition. At the council fire, all the spirits of the grandmothers and grandfathers crowd around. It is very common for a spirit to enter into someone at the council fire. It is a gift to be visited by the spirit of Heyoka."

He laughed. We laughed together.

There are tears for things, as I've been saying. There are also laughs. When we can free ourselves to feel these emotions spontaneously, I think we are more peaceful people, operating from the center of our real personalities rather than from wearisome social facades. And I think that storytelling is a healing and peacemaking art. Larry's story healed my sense of shame and gathered me back to the council fire. If we can work this ritual magic in the classroom, I think we will be "doing nonviolence." And, on the other hand, I hope we can learn to bring to the dreary seriousness of political discussion some of the havoc of art.

Early writers on nonviolent discipline often compared it to a kind of "moral jiu-jitsu," as does Arnold Hall in his classic essay, "Training for Non-Violence." Hall's overview of the subject is worth quoting at length:

> Nonviolent resistance challenges and presently undermines an aggressor's violent values: he is at once taken by surprise, whereas a violent response would have confirmed his own purposes and intention. Under the new circumstances his instincts no longer tell him what he is to do: he has, at the very moment when he needs to be acting, to think, and his thinking is at once side-tracked into wonder and curiosity; he becomes almost two people instead of one, with the loss of concentration which that entails. If there are onlookers (near and far), he finds that their support is diminished if his violence is excessive when it is unopposed. And all the while he is being treated as it were with respect by his victim, which itself is an unsettling experience. His basic emotions of fear, anger and hatred are disturbed and neutralized (195).

If we contrast Hall's scenario with what actually happens at many "peace" demonstrations—most recently, we blundered through another series during the Gulf War—I'm afraid we often find nothing that juggles the mental categories of the adversary, unsettles, or moves the discussion to a new plane of vision. No jiu-jitsu, no unbalancing, very little respect. The roles are drearily predictable: there will be some guerilla theater; people will lie down, or sit down, and be dragged away by grunting police, and the whole thing will probably not even be carried on the ten o'clock news.

We carry on with these robotic gestures of protest, I guess, because such tactics worked for Gandhi; they worked for Martin Luther King. What we should imitate, perhaps, is not the actions but the *spirit* of Gandhi and King: do the unexpected. Be an artist. Be a comic.

It's interesting to note how certain of Arnold Hall's phrases reflect traditional aesthetic principles: being "sidetracked into wonder and curiosity" is an excellent definition of artistic response. It's what Artistotle hoped for on opening night.

Good art (and, in particular, good comedy) respects the participants, rearranges reality, opens new moral possibilities, disorients, and resolves contradictions. A good "protest" should do the same; otherwise, nobody is thinking, nothing is changed. It's bad art. Worse, it may be a species of violence. We in the peace community are always in danger of tumbling unconsciously into our shadow. Eleanore Price Mather, quoting Maurice Friedman, puts it this way: "Nonviolence in fact may be, and sometimes is, covert violence, apocalyptic rage, perfectionist intolerance" (91). I think we should be willing, as my Native American friends recommend, occasionally to *go coyote*. Some of the best peace activists I know are puppeteers, jugglers, and clowns. Some day I will not be here. I will be with them, in motley.

Five

Silence and Slow Time

*N*ot so long ago when I was a child, it was still possible to escape from school for long periods of time if you could manage to find yourself in the throes of some lengthy illness for which bedrest was the only cure. Malingering with a vaguely weak heart, as I had the good fortune to do, I could read and dream for weeks at a time. I would listen to "Our Gal Sunday" on the radio, forming pictures of the action in my mind. I would lie in the sun in an altered state brought on by illness and sensory deprivation, watching spiders spin their webs. I managed to achieve a condition of sufficient delicacy to keep me in for recess most of my school career, even though I got well enough to go back to classes. My socialization was imperfect, but that's probably all to the good, considering the state of society. I would never grasp the rules of volleyball.

Modern medicine has pretty well eliminated this excellent education in the land of counterpane, and even children who are lucky enough to be blessed with a convalescence usually spend it propped up in front of reruns of *Leave It to Beaver.*

I think we should figure out some ways of getting a bit of leisure and bedrest and staring out the window back into the educational experience. I realize this view runs counter to contemporary administrative and parental policy. Educators today seem obsessed with how much *more* children could be learning: we plan for more math, more languages, longer school days, school on Saturday, shortening of summer vacation. We parents rush our children to dance lessons, music lessons, soccer, and swimming while trying to keep up with the Russians and the Japanese.

What if we tried to keep up with the ants, as this one-time child tried to do:

> Pausing to watch them, I studied the form of their activity, wondering how much of their own pattern they were able to see for themselves . . . I knew that I was so large that, to them, I was invisible. . . . I was gigantic, huge—able at one glance to comprehend . . . the work of the whole colony (12).

Another child went to this early morning session:

> I was . . . between four and five years old. . . . My feet, with the favorite black shoes with silver buckles, were gradually hidden from sight until I stood ankle deep in gently swirling vapor. . . . Suddenly I seemed to see mist as a shimmering gossamer tissue and the harebells . . . seemed to shine with a brilliant fire. Somehow I understood that this was the living tissue of life itself, in which that which we call consciousness was imbedded . . . (32).

And this child merely stared out the second story:

> The trees between the house and the river—I was on a level with their topmost branches—were either poplars or silver birch, and green fields stretched away beyond the river to the far distance. . . . The scene was very beautiful, and quite suddenly I felt myself to be on the verge of a great revelation. It was as if I had stumbled unwittingly on a place where I was not expected and was about to be initiated into some wonderful mystery . . . (37).

I have quoted here from Edward Robinson's book *The Original Vision*, which is a study of the religious experiences of ordinary young children. That young people have a spiritual nature, that they have experienced "great initiation" and "wonderful mystery" is seldom taken seriously enough. I think that if we truly believed this to be the case, our teaching would change. Robinson's work suggests that very early on, children experience events of great spiritual importance that speak to them with an authority impregnable to any subsequent doses of positivist education:

> I knew what I knew (13).
>
> The vision has never left me. . . . Moreover, the whole of this experience has ever since formed a kind of reservoir of strength fed from an unseen source (33).
>
> . . . the recollection of it acts as a kind of tap root to springs of my life (36).

The question for me is how do we teach people who are profoundly, and even stubbornly, spiritual beings? I think we assume that spiritual beings is the *last* thing they are (because it is perhaps the last thing they will let us know).

Fishing

I do not think it is possible to absorb much of anything without silence and rest on either side of the learning, to *absorb* something so that the learner takes on the quality and coloration of the object of study and appropriates it into cell and synapse: knows it.

Louis Agassiz, the marine zoologist, used to give each of his students a fish on the first day of class; he'd tell them to go away and study it until they understood it. A few hours later, most students would return with their fish under control. Agassiz would interrogate then judge, "No, you don't know enough yet." This gentle dance would go on for weeks, months. At the end of term, those students knew a few fish very well, and they probably knew something about learning, which is even more important than knowing something about fish.

I wish I had the courage to teach poetry that way.

What You Can Learn from "Bad" Teaching

A new policy in our department says you have to make up a syllabus and put it on file with the department secretary at the beginning of each term in case you die or go insane and someone has to take over your class. It's hard for me to figure out in advance what I'm going to do every day of the semester because I learn by going where I have to go (The Theodore Roethke Memorial School of Pedagogy).

But I will do it. I'm dutiful, and I know that the illusion of order is comforting to students.

I'm glad, though, that no one made one of my favorite teachers, Teresa Toomey, C.S.J., file her syllabus. Some would say that by the time I took her course in college, Sister Teresa was past her prime, getting eccentric. She was supposed to teach us Art History from Prehistory to the Present. We spent weeks on primitive cave painting, then stalled on Giotto. Day after day we sat in a dark classroom, looking at the confusion of spears and torches in "The Kiss of Judas" until we knew it. *Knew* it. Later, lurking morosely in the positivist pews of great universities where I read the Gospel of John in first year Greek, it was Giotto that rose before my eyes. That confusion of spears, and that alone, opened the Greek text to me. Now I knew *two* things.

This nun having done her work, art stops short for me in the early fourteenth century. Somewhere, filed in some Platonic syllabus, lie Raphael's fat madonnas, but they are not for me: I do not *know* them. I suppose that is a loss. But I do know two things.

Flowering from Within

What if we were to take seriously the possibility that our students have a rich and authoritative inner life and tried to nourish it rather than negate it?

I, at least, have often negated it. I have allowed my lip to curl over Blake's angels, let my students understand in some subtle way that, of course, we were not going to take Wordsworth's metaphysical ideas seriously. I have repeated, as most of us tend to do, the abusive patterns of my own graduate training.

Recently at a colloquium on the *Meno*, my colleagues and I discussed Plato's idea that *education is remembering.* Or, rather, we did not discuss it. Taking our cues from the alpha wolf of our academic pack, a philosopher, we sneered at it. It clashed too much with our materialistic paradigm of the nature of things.

And yet, whether we consider Plato's idea as metaphor or complex statement of ontology, it's something for which we can find a fair amount of empirical support in our classrooms and playrooms. "I played the violin before I knew you," one of my precocious young friends told his mother. With certain students, one has the sense not of teaching but of *reminding:*

> *The bud*
> *stands for all things*
> *even for those things that don't flower,*
> *for everything flowers, from within, of self-blessing;*
> *though sometimes it is necessary*
> *to reteach a thing its loveliness . . .*
>
> —(Galway Kinnell, 9)

If we thought things were flowering from within of self-blessing, it would change the way we go about our work in the classroom. We might talk less, listen more, encourage more. We might give up the violence of forcing our students to conform to external standards instead of gently leading them to remember, each one, what he needs.

I'm not arguing here for a Platonic position on the transmigration of souls. I'm simply suggesting that we try not to evade the texts we teach. The last time I taught Wordsworth's "Ode: Intimations of Immortality"—feeling guilty, to be sure, over my part in trashing the *Meno*—I asked students to write about any experiences they might have had that reinforced Wordsworth's affirmation of the spiritual experience of childhood. These were business majors and football players, for the most part, in a required course—not honor students, not aesthetes. Yet fully two-thirds of them revealed an inner world of depth and complexity and wonder. They were *delighted* with the question; they wanted to talk for hours.

When I asked the same question about the same text to a group of adult learners a few weeks ago, one old man burst into tears: he had been waiting all his life, so he said, for someone to raise this issue.

Again, I have no position to stake out here, no interpretation of the data. If I had spent my retired childhood watching something more important than spiders, or had indeed managed to learn more than two things so far in my life—I would have more to say. We are trained (if not educated) to believe that intellectual honesty requires a sceptical outlook. Yet, as Simone Weil observes in her spiritual autobiography, having disciplined ourselves to say carefully, "Perhaps all that is not true,"—and without ceasing to say it—we need to learn to say also, "Perhaps all that is true" (19). The second motion of the mind is necessary to the integrity of the first.

Spending Time

If we try to look at education in terms of the spiritual inquiry of both teacher and student, it may be useful to retrieve the idea that literary study, in particular, is essentially a contemplative activity. Therefore, we have to look differently at how we spend our classroom time.

Perhaps we should teach fewer texts or shorter texts. Perhaps "English 300: Shakespeare" could deal with three plays instead of six or twelve. Perhaps the *Iliad* is worth half a semester. Maybe we could read aloud more in the classroom because there is something significant in learners' simultaneous experience of an important text. In doing this, one feels a connection to the great central traditions of scholarship: Talmudic, Zen, monastic. I think we need to center ourselves in spiritual tradition if we are to survive the wilderness of the American school system. If we are not grounded in some tradition of values, we are grounded in the tradition of no-values. Speeding through a book a week, what philosophical systems frame our work? Pragmatism. Sophistry. Materialism. We are *using* texts rather than entering into them. We act without reverence for the word. Last year's paperbacks decompose on our shelves; we have no *use* for them.

White Space

It requires a long time to take in a few words.

On either side of the word we need a patch of white, of silence, like the white space that defines a Chinese painting, or the rests in music that permit the notes to be heard.

By and large, our students are relentlessly overstimulated. They sing the body electric: plugged in, tuned out, motorized. And we are overstimulated, too. Many of us hate silence, especially in the classroom. It is the teacher's ultimate nightmare: what if I can't fill fifty minutes? And yet, if students spend twenty minutes in silence looking at ten lines of Homer, it can be time well spent.

I heard a student talking the other day about the difference between two sociology professors. "I love Professor Jones. He lectures from the moment he enters the room, without ever looking at his notes. You really get your money's worth in there. I don't know about Professor Smith. Sometimes you ask him a question and he looks out the window for a while before he answers."

I think this student has confused education with the drive-through line at McDonald's, but can you blame him; for, so has Professor Jones.

Teaching in the Fast Lane

I wonder why we sometimes teach as though we did not want students to grasp the implications of what they are "learning." We handle texts like precious vessels that must be handed down from parent to child but that must on no account truly be opened: there are genii inside, unpredictable spirits, dangerous to the countryside. Some kind of recombinant DNA.

Teachers often pride themselves on a challenging syllabus, which usually means that they assign an astonishing amount of reading. Students perceive this as a "tough" course and the teacher a "tough" teacher. Everybody is happy—parents, principals, deans, school boards, even students, who share in the universal need to succeed at something "tough."

Thus, the average college curriculum comes to look like one of those European tours that advertises ten countries in two weeks. At best, what you get out of that is the educational equivalent of cocktail party chatter. Worse, faced with an impossible syllabus, students may fall into the habit of moral evasion. They pretend to know, they pretend to be asleep or dead, they bone up on yellow-bellied plot summaries, they plagiarize.

Let us look for a moment from the beginner's point of view at what it means to study a difficult text. You must enter into the world of the author, into an alien culture with strange customs and ways of thinking. You must master a new vocabulary without sufficient time to look up the words, many of which are not in the dictionary anyway. You will read at a breakneck pace, trying to grasp, at minimum, the plot. You will come to class, frozen with terror, for the teacher can ask you any question about any part of the text at any moment. What do you know about the *Iliad*? It's about Greece. But that will not satisfy the professor. "What is Achilles's problem?" she will say. Not his literal, vulgar problem. Not the mere plot-level problem—his problem on the philosophical level? Come on now, kids, we've only got four days on this text and you should already be reading Aristotle for next week."

After a while, if you act dumb enough, or dead enough, you will train the teacher to leave you in peace. Hating silence as she does, she will fall into lecturing, and you can just write it all blessedly down. Soon you'll discover you don't need to read the texts at all. Your professor will slump over lunch with her colleagues saying, "I tried discussion, but it just doesn't work. They don't care. I don't think half of them bother to open the books."

You will leave your study of the *Iliad* with some bizarre notes on The Heroic Ideal, about emergence from mythic undifferentiation to post-tribal self-consciousness. Does that make any sense? Who cares? It's in your notes.

Maybe you have some questions, but surely they can't be relevant. After a while it's less painful not to have questions. At least you've done Homer, and you can say so at any cocktail party.

Silencing the Text

My friend and colleague, Jim Vopat, used to talk about facing the consequences of what we teach. Often we don't face the texts, but rather, we do everything we can to silence them. Most great literature is so radical, it takes its knife so near the bone, that we sometimes don't want to deal with it.

It is dangerous to stand in a classroom with literature in our hands. What do we do with those awful moments in Virginia Woolf when her meaning becomes unmistakable: there is no possibility of human beings understanding each other, no hope at all. When one discovers in the middle of *The Bacchae*, that, yes, sometimes mothers want to tear their sons limb from limb. How many questions do we dare to ask about things like this? And will they be on The Test?

It's no wonder that the more sensitive among us run screaming to graduate school for some kind of vaccination. And we get it. In graduate school a new formula takes hold: quadruple the number of texts you read, halve your time again because you are now a teaching assistant and probably trying to raise a family on the side. With luck, you can learn never to have time to think about what you are reading. In case you haven't learned it already, this is your last chance to discover that it isn't essential to read the damn books at all; what's important is to know what the latest academic superstar had to say.

One of Robertson Davies's characters, a musician, angrily rejects his student's naive comment about how "educational" her lessons with him have been:

> What we are doing isn't really educational. It's enlightening, I suppose, and its purpose is to nurture the spirit. If formal education has any bearing on the arts at all, its purpose is to make critics, not artists. Its usual effect is to cage the spirit in other peoples' ideas—the ideas of poets and philosophers, which were once splendid insights into the nature of life, but which people who have no insights of their own have hardened into dogmas. It is the spirit we must work with, and not the mind itself. For 'the spirit searcheth all things, yea, the deep things of God' (593).

How, indeed, can we work with the spirit and not the mind itself? This, it seems to me, is the central goal of any teaching practice concerned with the inner world.

First of all, we must stop trying to cover so much material. What's the matter with these teachers who are constantly agonizing in the lunchroom about how they have fallen behind their syllabus? They must have been cruelly toilet trained. How many novels do you have to read to establish the fact that there was, indeed, a Victorian period?

We need to keep in mind the process our students are going through as they desperately try to grasp the customs and mores of these alien worlds. If we assign a hundred pages of reading in a night, they will do no more than grasp the most superficial impression. They will come to class empty with no ideas of their own, ready for us to feed them a mash of the latest critic, like those birds who regurgitate for their young.

It is only on a second or third reading, as we all know in our hearts, that we begin to get the point. Why do we make it well-nigh impossible for our students—and often for ourselves—to have this experience? Nothing else that needs to be done is as important as this is. But we often do not allow time; we try to keep up with the syllabus. No wonder so many freshmen leave their required course with the idea that literature is an arcane mystery they never could "get."

Perhaps we silence the texts for our students because, in our pain, we have long ago silenced them for ourselves. While students are curling up with *Cliff's Notes*, is the professor rereading *Mrs. Dalloway*? I fear not. With committee meetings to attend, advisees to counsel, papers to grade, and private lives to screw up at our leisure, it's hard to find time to read. In any case, we do not trust our own readings. We learned that in graduate school, if not before.

Doing Nothing

In teaching, as in other kinds of spiritual guidance, it is often best to do nothing. But at the same time that one is doing nothing, one can act with a very precise and focused attention.

If I intervene, for example, in a writing group which has broken down, I take away the power of individuals to find a solution. Perhaps it's wiser to do nothing. But while you are doing nothing, you have to be present in the situation in a contemplative way and lend it your strength. I have no idea why this "works," or whether the principles involved are physical or metaphysical; I'm told that in post-Newtonian physics, the mere act of observation changes the course of atoms. So what? I don't know. I'm only reporting phenomena.

There is a great deal of difference between not caring or being lazy and doing nothing in a serious way. Perfect

NOTHING has a quality of PRESENCE, like certain rests in music. The secret is to be *there* and not someplace else, and if you are really present, the right action will follow. If I am not *there*, all the fixes I know will be the wrong fixes. I relearn this ten times a week, crashing around and doing damage. The part of me that wants to show off and be heroic, which is the dominant part of me, fiddles with things and leaves behind a dance of chaos.

Perhaps I am suggesting something like the Taoist concept of non-doing, which, Westerners often misconstrue as a sort of passive opting-out. Lao-Tzu did not teach non-striving but rather, "striving through the power of the Inner Life," as Isabella Mears notes in her translation of the *Tao Te Ching* (5–6).

It helps me to remember that natural systems tend to be self-correcting. When we let people fix themselves, assisting them only with a kind of friendly regard while they find their strength, we allow them their inborn power.

I think we need to balance the words *try* and *let* in our minds. We should try a little, but we should let as well. Most of us, because we are perfectionists and the products of abusive education, *try* too hard and *let* not at all. We think that what we do not do ourselves does not happen.

If you "let" your students fix themselves, of course they may not thank you. You will probably not be Teacher of the Year. Our need for approval makes non-action particularly difficult. My urge to fix and change is driven relentlessly by Ego, that screaming predator.

It is often best to do nothing, but it is not *always* best to do nothing. Knowing when to *try* and when to *let* involves a complicated process of discernment. I suppose that's why, on the whole, it's a good thing for a teacher, too, to have some kind of inner life.

Six

The Dancing Is Difficult

"Great artists," Margot Fonteyn once said "are people who find the way to be themselves in their art. Any sort of pretension induces mediocrity in art and life alike" (Bernheimer, 2F).

Another teacher and I got to talking about authority in the classroom, especially with respect to the problems of first-year teachers. "If you are idealistic," said Karen, "and only idealistic people go into the profession, you want to be kind and approachable. My daughter, in her first year of teaching, tried hard to be good and loving toward students, but the ninth graders just tore her apart."

Karen and I agree that there is a mysterious quality—call it authority—which, if you have it, you can do as you like, and if you don't, you can't tie your shoes.

"I gave her the standard advice," Karen continued, "if you don't have it, act as if you have it. But she felt this was being hypocritical. . . ."

Having authority as a teacher is rather like finding your voice as a writer. Maybe at certain stages you have to try on a lot of masks until you find one that fits your face, or until you feel comfortable appearing without one (and strong enough to take the consequences). Very few of us are, at twenty-one, sufficiently integrated spiritually and emotionally to do the job. Very few of us have, at any age, enough emotional or spiritual safety to respond with absolute authenticity in all situations. We grasp instead at the patterned response, one that reduces anxiety, like "acting as if you have it."

Such poses are like water wings; they hold us somewhere between swimming and drowning. But do you want to stay in that place your whole career? Some teachers "act as if" all their lives long, never winning through to the pleasure of being themselves. They can be effective, too, within a limited cultural framework. Fonteyn also said—she who was so widely praised for the emotional nuances of her work—"the acting is easy. The dancing is difficult" (Bernheimer, 2F).

The dancing, in fact, takes courage and wisdom. It takes courage to discard a patterned response, wisdom to hold on to a mask you really need. What happens if you let all your vulnerability show? I don't know; if you have had experience along these lines, write me a letter from whatever hospital you are in. The best we can do is to be conscious about our choices, keep distinguishing in our own minds between the mask and the face: today I will pretend this much, risk this much. Aim to pretend less and less, but don't outrun your strength.

Well, wait a minute; that's pretty stupid advice. I'm tempted to delete the last two sentences, but I will leave them in place as a warning to anyone innocent enough to take in anything I have written before sitting a long while with head cocked, like my dog, Shep, exploring the wonders of the phenomenal world (or barking at it a good length of time, as a different dog might do).

Because, of course, if this shape-shifting among the roles we play were conscious, it would trouble us very little. If we could get up in the morning and dress for a calculated amount of pretending, how quickly we could get out of the house. But I, for one, often dither in front of the mental closet, wondering who I am today or who I might be by noon.

One of my advanced writing assignments goes like this:

> List as quickly as you can all the different characters who make up who you are. You can list them by name, if the names come quickly to you (i.e., "Sam the Whiner") or by characteristics

("nice Baptist girl") or simply as "the one who . . ." ("the one who always tells me to take a nap").

The younger and more inexperienced the students, the more they resist this exercise because they need to believe, for whatever developmental reasons, that personality is univocal. Adult students, by contrast, will rapidly sketch out the inner players and be able to tell each other who has the power, who has all the lines, who never gets heard, who is the internal critic, who their friends like best, who sounds like the inward teacher—and all the other questions we can bring to bear on this exercise in "voice." I have come to believe, therefore, that as we grow toward maturity, we become more comfortable with the polyphrenia of our inner world. Still I, for my part, cannot always distinguish between the mask and the face or manipulate the mummers' roles I play.

In practice, then, the issue is perhaps this: to what extent can I give my personality full range in the classroom? Thomas Kelly, a writer well known in Quaker circles, often wrote about the pain of the divided self and, by contrast, the whimsical option of living from consensus of an inner committee (115). Our culture exerts considerable pressure on professional people to be a certain kind of person; marginal styles (gay, black, female, etc.) are routinely extinguished by the ruthless behaviorism of professional life. (The stress of our subsequent straight-white-male role-playing is murderous—probably even for straight white males). But students learn a lot from seeing the breadth of response it's possible to make in the life of the mind/heart.

Can we separate the acting from the dancing (or the dancer from the dance)? The question, once again, implies a process that has all the crazy contradictions of any spiritual discipline. In teaching, in learning, we find something out only to meet its perfect contradiction the next day. We keep pushing through oppositions to a new synthesis, and then we lose the synthesis. It takes courage to go on with it. The whole process of serious thinking, approached honestly, can be fiercely painful. A while ago, for example, in my freshman Texts and Traditions course, I put the group in a circle to answer a question one student had raised: What is the authority of this text? (Plato, *Republic*, Book VII) By what criteria could we say it is "true" or "untrue"; in what sense could we "believe" or "disbelieve" it?

Since the course met right before lunch, hands were waving before a minute-and-a-half had passed—they wanted to get out of there. It came to me that, whatever they thought the answer was, it might be important to analyze our process of questioning.

"How do you feel when you think you have the right answer?" I asked.

"Great! Wonderful!" they responded. (Halfway to lunch.)

"And what would tell you that maybe your answer is wrong or incomplete?"

One young woman responded, "It would feel like a mouse kind of gnawing at the back of my mind." She was beginning to feel the sharp teeth. Others described a kind of restlessness or discomfort.

I pursued the point. "How does it make you feel when you realize you don't have a good answer?"

"Frustrated!"

"Desperate!!!"

This exchange helped me to understand something about my own learning, as well as demonstrating the blocks immature learners face as they fumble rather desperately for "right answers," "better ideas," "ideas that will get A's"—ideas, even, that will resolve some of the pain of their own search.

We talked, then, about the courage we need to have to put aside the phony euphoria we feel when the answer seems right but isn't, the courage to plunge into the feelings of frustration and desperation in search of a better, truer idea. Often in teaching I'm reminded of the Buddhist concept of the Great Warrior, the hero of the inner world, for I think we are asking our students to do a brave thing. And it is important to put this idea before young people because it appeals to their idealism and spirit. We all like to do something brave. (If *we* do not call to their idealism and power of self-transcendence, the military recruiters will.)

If we are being honest and attentive, I think there is always a place of discomfort in our teaching practice, a place of incongruity between our beliefs and our conduct. For many years I ignored that raw spot in myself; in fact, I am good at ignoring it. All the years I lectured, all the years I dressed for success, every time I bleated mindlessly about the latest French critic, I was ignoring it. I can ignore disruptive feelings until I get physically ill. The year after my sabbatical in that contemplative Quaker community that rewired my brain for tolerating silence and slow time, I came back to school, picked up lecturing where I had left off, and almost passed out on the floor. That year, every time I would start to lecture, my chest would cramp and I wouldn't be able to breathe.

I can take little personal credit, then, for seeking a way to be myself in my art, since it seemed to be a choice between that and asphyxiation. Later I remembered a similar incident in Augustine's *Confessions*, which occurred while Augustine was resisting his deepest understanding of his life's work: ". . . my lungs had begun to give way as the result of overwork in teaching. I found it difficult to breathe deeply . . ." (186). Clearly this kind of metaphysical seizure must be an occupational hazard of rhetoric teachers. Augustine finally resolved to leave the profession: ". . . I would gently withdraw from a position where I was making use of my tongue in the talking-shop; no longer would my students . . . buy from my mouth material for arming their own madness" (185).

The reader may sense a contradiction here between my earlier discussion of the ease and grace that accompany good practice in teaching and this portrayal of life-threatening difficulty. I can't explain the paradox, or why we must learn again and again to arm ourselves for heroic effort in order to learn that the trick is letting go. When a great artist explains it, of course it's always very simple. This is how Margot

Fonteyn described her career: "I'd say Fonteyn had a good line. With that she was able to go on. . . . Her back was rather strong. That helped hold her together. I'd say she listened to the music" (Bernheimer, 2F).

What Nanny Really Meant

Similar to the process of finding a way to be oneself in teaching is learning to affirm the authority of one's own readings. This is particularly difficult in an era when it has become more important to master criticism than to read literature. Yet, as W. H. Auden has observed, scholarly arguments are mostly

> *. . . anent*
> *What Nannie really meant (45).*

So let's trust our readings, and let's be bravely clear about where those readings come from. Literary study is not a very objective business. What we often see in literary texts is our own life patterns writ larger and better than we could write them ourselves. We are drawn to certain authors and fields of study because, unconsciously perhaps, they help us to sort out our own concerns. One of the best things a practicing critic can do for her psychological well-being is to turn a cool eye from time to time on her work and say, "What are the recurring patterns here? What seems to have an emphasis out of proportion to its intrinsic weight? And what does this say about the critic?"

Sometimes our students are kind enough to do this for us, as one of mine recently did at the end of class:

"Professor O'Reilley, I have taken four courses from you, and I've observed that you are obsessed with the dialogue between the rational and intuitive in Joseph Conrad."

"Surely *obsessed* is too strong a word, Patrick."

"But I don't see any such pattern. I think you made it all up."

"Well, hang on," I say, always resisting self-knowledge. "Next week we'll talk about pacifism in *Lord Jim*, or maybe about Conrad's assault on patriarchy . . ."

I've travelled a little in the academic communities of England, Australia, and New Zealand where English teachers seem less defensive about the subjectivity of their discipline and appear to take the good-natured abuse of their colleagues more in stride. "Oh, you teach English," an Australian historian once said to me. "That's all wanking."

Well, a lot of it is. I do not intend to suggest, however, that if one is writing about mothers and daughters in Virginia Woolf, such criticism reflects merely one's own issues and not Woolf's. What I mean is something much more encouraging and hopeful: that our own life experiences give each of us a unique way in to literary texts; that, indeed, all great critical readings are made possible because of a critic's being alerted to a certain issue by his or her own experience. Consider, as an example, Professor Harold Goddard's remarkable, posthumously published, essay on *The Turn of the Screw* written about 1920, which anticipated a major shift in our understanding of the story. Goddard disingenuously admitted that his reading came out of "a remarkable parallelism between a strange passage in my own early experience . . . and what I conceived to be the situation in *The Turn of the Screw*" (184). Goddard's memory of an unreliable governess sensitized him to the possibility that the governess in James's story was not to be trusted. Here is literal inquiry into what Nanny meant.

I do not believe objectivity is without merit, nor is it impossible to achieve, especially if we think of it as a meditative state of benevolent observation that comes of having transcended one's own drama. Nor do I subscribe to the recurrent undergraduate fantasy that a text means whatever you want it to mean. There are rules governing the verification of a literary thesis, the same as there are rules governing the verification of an hypothesis in science. But one of the best reasons to study literature is to engage our own experience in a dialogue with it. We need to watch our drama in order to transcend it.

As though art were a sort of mystical transformation, William Carlos Williams writes, that it "... reveal[s] the oneness of experience; it rouses rather than stupefies the intelligence by demonstrating the importance of personality, by showing the individual ... that his life is valuable—when completed by the imagination" (107).

Vulnerable as we may feel, we need to stand in our own lives as we read, as we teach, and as we teach our students to read and interpret. Making a similar point, Parker Palmer compares the classroom to Quaker worship:

> We prepare for a meeting for learning by trying to become vulnerable to both hurt and healing in others and in ourselves ... Whatever the subject of study in the classroom, the shadow subject is ourselves, our limits, our potentials. As long as that remains in the shadows, it will block both individual and group from full illumination. But if both hurt and self-doubt can be brought into the light ... then learning will flower (5).

Palmer's proposal challenges us radically: few of us are able or willing to disarm ourselves to the degree he suggests. I, with my chilly northern character, have failed this test repeatedly. Palmer's scenario also presupposes a fair amount of maturity on the part of the group. I am told—though, frankly, I have never seen it—that it is the natural impulse of adolescents to attack the vulnerable and go for the throat. These folktales make us cautious.

But in my many years of teaching I have known few students incapable of concern and support for the hurts of others. As teachers we see a pretty broad spectrum of "average" humanity, and, from my vantage point at least, average people are capable of splendid feats of sensitivity and altruism. Still, you have to keep your eye out for the occasional sociopath.

Is it possible to be "vulnerable to hurt and healing" and still protect one's limits of comfort in a professional situation? I think so. Let's assume you are a rather private person. You are not willing to tell students that your cat died this morning; you do not want to hear about their dead cats. I think, however, that the best kind of teaching comes out of a willingness to stand in one's own condition. The best teaching does not come out of dropping your feelings at the classroom door. You don't need to *talk* about being sad or happy, you just need to be present to your own inward life. It's an attitude of mind, a quality of attention.

Reader response theory has taught us a number of useful ways to help students bring some degree of affective attention to the text. It encourages us to look at memories, fantasies, and personal associations as we read, to write journal exercises that keep these inner visions in a dialectical relationship with the text. None of this personal material need come into class discussion or essay writing. But I think it may if one chooses. The personal context keeps us grounded in the real. It puts a little more at stake, and that is good because in the average classroom there is not enough at stake. And that is not worth our time. It is not worth our lives.

Seven

The Retro War

*L*ike one of our brutal Minnesota winter blizzards, the Persian Gulf War blew up one January day and buried our hope that the world was evolving with any rapidity toward a peaceable future. My son told me he was thinking seriously about joining the air force; he didn't think it was fair for privileged white people to sit on the side lines as his father's generation (he thought) had done.

"Are you for the war?" I heard our returning students greet each other over and over as the new semester began. I never heard no. Nor did I hear a lot of enthusiastic, gung-ho yeses. Just the occasional subdued and cautious yes. Working from the government's latest public relations spin, they found the Gulf War to be within the guidelines of "Just War." (Or, as Colman McCarthy calls it "Just Slaughter.") This is not your father's war, they perceived. This is your grandfather's war. The good one.

Young people—and I speak now for the rather conservative but thoughtful ones I teach—seem to be looking for moral regeneration. First it was preppy haircuts, then the retro war: a war that made a brief, crazy claim to restore a sense of national purpose.

One mother's story caught the absurdity of it all: "My son went to visit his high school buddy in the army—he saw that drawer full of underwear, all folded in triangles—and he enlisted." That's a short poem, it seems to me, about the longing for order and discipline that pulls the strings of our young. They want their lives to mean something; they want someone to make them organize their drawers. At an even higher level than housekeeping, "the service" represents for many an ideal of self-transcendence.

Today's young have many reasons to go to war that were not listed in my handbook for conscientious objectors: solidarity, self-purification, and the post-feminist desire to reclaim a traditional sense of manhood—even the simple need to care for and cherish something. One day I saw one of my ROTC students, in black beret and camouflage, cradling gently what I thought must be a puppy. As he came near, I could see that it was the American flag. I wish we could give our young people something even more holy to cherish.

During those days of the Gulf War, with CNN blasting at me from all sides, I tried to rethink the austere and lonely terrain of peace testimony. I have no truck with Just War Theory; I am trying to figure out an ideal of absolute, radical nonviolence (failing it on an hourly basis) and *I don't even know why I am doing this.* In my middle years I write in the spirit of those letters exchanged by Daniel Berrigan and Thomas Merton when they called themselves "burnt men." They couldn't seem to remember why they had chosen their paths. They couldn't remember, but they were hanging on like Annie Dillard's famous weasel.

And so was I. I kept asking my friends in the peace movement, "Why do we profess nonviolence? Because Jesus lived this testimony? Because Gandhi did? Because, as Mammy Yoakam used to say, good is better than evil because it's nicer?"

I became a pacifist for the reasons I wrote about earlier, because of discovering the link between classroom teaching and Vietnam, because of the hawk shadows on the prairie of my childhood and—as I remembered in January of 1991—because I didn't want my son (a newborn when I made those first decisive steps into a Quaker meeting house) to go to war. That was not a good reason—or, if it was a good reason, it was not one that could in any way bind him. We create ourselves, Kierkegaard said, by our choices. I wrote that down in my college philosophy class, but so did my son. He, along with my students, was warning me that pacifists as well as generals tend to fight the last war.

My favorite photo of my father sits before me as I write. He is twenty. He wears his Air Force cap and earphones, his brown leather pilot's jacket. As the Gulf War began, he was in the last months of his life and coming into the tenderness that often grows on strong men as they age. He called, full of emotion, to talk to his grandson. He said to me, "I've been watching all this on TV, the bombing raids and all, and I was remembering—I just wanted to tell him—don't enlist."

Our American part in the Gulf War was over quickly (if indeed it is over). And now we hear the stories of rape and torture on both sides, the lies retold and recanted; we ponder the usefulness of the action. A new generation wakes up to learn that its passions may have been trifled with, as my father's were. "Never such innocence again," as Philip Larkin said ("MCMXIV, 28") of the generation that fought World War I—and of us.

An Ecstasy of Fumbling

During the Gulf War—asking myself relentlessly, "Why am I doing this?"—I remembered Tony Donato, whom I took care of twenty-five years ago when I was a college student volunteering at a veteran's hospital. Tony was an old man; he had been gassed in World War I and had lived in the VA ever since. Usually he sat in his wheel chair in a corner of the ward, staring at nothing much through his old-fashioned steel-rimmed spectacles, unresponsive and docile. But every so often, once a week or so, he would come to "life." He would scream and cower and try to defend himself. He was back in the war, stuck, trapped in history.

"Who are these? Why sit they here in twilight?" Wilfred Owen asks in his poem, "Mental Cases," written in 1918, the year Tony came to live at the veteran's hospital. Owen replies:

> *These are men whose minds the Dead have ravished.*
> *Memory fingers in their hair of murders,*
> *Multitudinous murders they once witnessed*
> . . . .
> *Always they see these things and hear them . . .* (69)

The ward I worked on was bluntly called a "terminal ward." They hadn't managed to come up with a euphemism that covered all the various finalities that trapped men there for months, years, or a whole lifetime: head injuries, paralysis, the consequences of mustard gas. But there was a kind of gallows humor and animal respect for each other that always operated among the men and the nurses in the ward. (In all my time there, I never saw a doctor: "Nobody is sick, we are all dead, ha ha," the guys would say.) Many were in what's now called a "persistent vegetative state," but we did not recognize that category then. Although some men could not speak or hear or move, each seemed to contribute to the community, each had a place and even a peer evaluation: one semi-comatose patient might be "a mean bastard" in the ward's judgment, another "a real clown." Tony Donato was "OK." Tony was "a good old boy."

My usual job was to feed Tony his puréed baby food. That was before they invented feeding tubes and relieved nursing staffs of volumes of work per meal. Or maybe they had the technology but thought it was too cruel to use. Maybe they thought the ancient personal rituals of feeding and wiping drool and giving drinking water to the "terminal" case had some value beyond efficiency. Unless he was having a hard time back in the war, Tony could manage to eat at his own pace. It took him an hour or so. On a bad day, he would cry and choke, sending waves of misery through the ward.

"What are you feeding that poor old stiff?" Wally, the fat king of the terminal ward would yell. Wally was paralyzed from the neck down, but nothing had reduced the volume of his evening news and commentary. Catching maybe the scent of chopped liver, "Cat food!" he would judge. "Spit it out, Tony. Be a man."

Often Wally could make Tony laugh and bring him back from Ypres or wherever he was pinned. It was a delicate balance because laughter could also make him choke. And so we went on.

That terrible things happen to innocent people is not the best reason to become a pacifist. (Terrible things happen sometimes because we do not go to war.) As the years went by, I found better reasons, but at least until my son was born, there was no reason that held my heart's attention like the case of Tony Donato. When I was little someone showed me a piece of amber that held the carcass of a fly, and I used to ponder the strange convergences that froze forever that insect in stone. It was not that I had a soft spot in my heart for flies. Even at seven, it was clear to me that we could slip our strings of safety and be lost.

"Gas! GAS! Quick, boys!"—Owen writes in "Dulce et Decorum Est":

> *An ecstasy of fumbling,*
> *Fitting the clumsy helmets just in time,*
> *But someone still was yelling out and stumbling*
> *And floundering like a man in fire or lime.—*
> *Dim through the misty panes and thick green light,*
> *As under a green sea, I saw him drowning (55).*

Coming from an air force family, I have always respected the men and women who, as we say, "serve." There are few chances in the modern world to transcend our selfish interests, and all of us want desperately for our lives to count. That's why I hear young people say that they want to join the army so their lives will mean something. I find this touching and a perverse commentary on the way our society respects and challenges the altruism of its youth.

I want Tony Donato's life, a life lived in quotation marks, to count. That is why I can't stop telling this story.

Eight

The Sibyl in the Bottle

I've been talking about facing the consequences of what we teach. In these chapters, I've been trying to face the consequences of one particular course in war literature, exploring what it has to say about the nature of the human species. Let me remind you that we discovered in that class certain recurring patterns in war literature: a disrupted relationship with nature, loss of faith in any transcendent structure of meaning, progressive mechanization of the formerly human world, and a severing of ties between men and women. We realized, finally (replicating Paul Fussell's thesis), that these patterns make up a definition of being human in our time. I have suggested that since this climate of alienation seems to result from a century of war, it can be addressed by nonviolent discipline, and that it *is* being addressed by nonviolent discipline in our classrooms, if we choose to think about our teaching in that way.

As I try to bring various threads of this narrative together, I am searching for a useful—if not an ultimate—synthesis. Ten years ago when I began thinking about these things, feminism was my "unified field theory." I had hopes that what then seemed a foreseeable triumph of inclusivist values would bring all of us, multicultural / male / female / gay / straight into the peaceable kingdom. Indeed, two writers who have had a pervasive influence on my approach to teaching, Peter Elbow and Parker Palmer, have developed much of their work in light of the early feminist analysis.

To tie feminism to "inclusivist" values is to frame the women's movement in a way that relatively few contemporary scholars in the field would countenance today. In the late 1970s, however, when my friends and I started talking about feminist pedagogy, we defined it in terms of collaboration, empathy, multivocalism, personal narration, and so on. By exploring these modes we hoped to liberate the voices not only of women but of anyone who had been traditionally discredited in a community that valued only competition, logical analysis, univocal argument, and objective narration. Our intention (but perhaps I should speak only for myself) was not to exclude traditional rhetorical strategies but to broaden their range. Such a philosophy might have been derived from *In a Different Voice* or *Women's Ways of Knowing*, or it might not. A Buddhist scholar might devise similar classroom strategies, as might someone from a tribal culture, or any freckled suburban kid who felt, for whatever reason, out of sync with the dominant style.

But back then we located our critique in what we called feminism, and we believed that feminism demanded an address to the dislocations defined above: that it implied respect for the natural world, a retrieval of spiritual values, and the primacy of the personal. In war literature—to return again to that paradigm—the rejection of these values is often, as though instinctively, conjoined with separation from or destruction of the feminine. In his prototypic novel *The Red Badge of Courage*, for example, Stephen Crane leads Henry Fleming away from home, mother, and girlfriend, through progressive enslavement to the toys of war and alienation from maternal Nature, whom he conceives as "a woman with a deep aversion to tragedy" (41). This is the warrior's archetypal journey. War literature relentlessly repeats these patterns of rupture from the maternal, natural, and feminine. In our time, however, the American hero, can no longer, like Huck Finn, "light out" for the open spaces. Nature has closed her green doors. In *Catch 22*, Yossarian's woods are haunted by a madman. The taciturn hero of *A Farewell to*

Arms tries to retreat into the mountains with his sweetheart, but she dies attempting the inappropriate wartime activity of giving birth.

In order to wage war, these texts suggest, it is necessary to throttle the feminine—the living woman who gets in your way or the anima within. At the beginning of *The Waste Land*, which is among other things, an important war poem, T. S. Eliot sets the figure of the Cumaean sybil—an image of the feminine spiritual and prophetic principal—suspended in a bottle, crying for death. I think she is a central image of humankind in our century.

From its beginnings, literature has warned us of the danger of suppressing the feminine, either because, as in Euripedes' *The Bacchae*, these repressed instincts will turn on us and tear us to pieces, or, as Sophocles in one of his most prophetic moments says, the earth has only so much to give, and the drive to civilize and cultivate risks the ultimate exhaustion of the eco-system:

> *Many the wonders but nothing walks stranger than man.*
> *This thing crosses the sea in the winter's storm,*
> *making his path through the roaring waves.*
> *and she, the greatest of gods, the earth—*
> *ageless she is and unwearied—he wears her away*
> *as the plows go up and down from year to year*
> *and his mules turn up the soil.*
>
> —(*Antigone*, 87)

This is not a message that our leaders have always wanted to incorporate into their energy policies, nor is it a message that women (even) have paid sufficient attention to. Now that some people *have* noticed, many others do not want to. (I still hear classicists describe Sophocles's choral ode as a "hymn to man," without any understanding of an ironic undercurrent.)

From the point of view of the English teacher looking at issues of peace and justice, feminism has called our attention to the different and sometimes divergent ways men and women read and notice things in a text. Women students are more likely to notice female characters, of course. They also tend to pay attention to the marginalized and unprotected. In a recent discussion group I attended on the literature of the Trojan War, the men wanted to talk about Achilles; the women wanted to look at issues of power and oppression. Women wanted to know why the baby was thrown over the wall. Our concern with "women's issues" annoyed the men, and they tended to brush off our comments as though we had proposed a discussion of fashion in togas. "Look here," one of them finally said, "there is nothing personal in this, it's just that historical consensus has determined the important questions in this area are questions about Achilles."

The following point is so obvious that I would not bother restating it, except that I seem to have to do so at every turn in academic life: what we call "historical consensus" all too often reflects the judgment calls of people in power, usually men; critical canons are formulated by winners; what is and is not an important question is determined by those with the most clout. The women in my classes, by contrast, tend to raise the issues of people on the edges: issues of racism, imperialism, sexism, homophobia, and violence, problems that the powerful have not felt in their bodies and hence dismiss as "unimportant." (Similarly, it took a black male student to "read" me the racial subtext of *Othello*, a subtext I was once inclined to exclude from critical consideration.)

In her interpretation of the myth of Demeter, the Jungian analyst Nor Hall writes: "There is a void felt these days by women—and men—who suspect that their feminine nature, like Persephone, has gone to hell." The cure of an emotional wound, she goes on to say, is in the wound itself, and so "the female void cannot be cured by conjunction with the male, but rather by an internal conjunction, by an integration of its own parts, by a remembering of or putting back together of the mother-daughter body" (68).

Women are remembering, but it is hard. Our own stories have been lost to us, and we are trying to put things together from shards swept to the edges of the male world. We are searching for the bits and pieces of somebody's memory of who we are. This is why women's texts are important to us, especially the work of women who, like Alice Walker, seem to know the location of the forgotten gardens:

> ... one day when I was sitting quiet and feeling like a motherless child, which I was, it come to me: that feeling of being part of everything, not separate at all. I knew that if I cut a tree, my arm would bleed ... (203).

It is frightening to contemplate the vulnerability of this connected world, which is not only the garden of women but also the sanctuary of spirit. The sacred sites of the heart are no match for the great earth movers growling outside my window as I write this: Native American holy places, razed for a shopping mall, African-American church communities, diners, and barbershops leveled for a freeway eight blocks from where I write.

Women have traditionally valued such private spaces, sacred to connection, and the white male power structure has not. Walker says,

> You have to get man off your eyeball, before you can see anything a'tall. Man corrupt everything.... He on your box of grits, in your head, all over the radio. He try to make you think he everywhere. Soon as you think he everywhere, you think he God. But he ain't. Whenever you trying to pray, and man plop himself on the other end of it, tell him to git lost.... Conjure up flowers, wind, water, a big rock (204).

What's interesting about this passage—and one could cite many others like it from the works of contemporary writers who come from a background of racial, gender, or class oppression—is how many different issues it raises. It is not only about feminism but about a democratized mysticism, racial justice, and the conjure-power of nature. It calls us to account to the inclusive agenda of the anima.

I think we should look at texts like Walker's, as well as at texts like the *Iliad*, rather as an archaeologist looks at bits of pottery, expecting that the patterning of the fragment will give us a clue to the nature of the whole. What is this culture like? Where has it been? Where is it going? As we turn over such material, we might see both a warning and a solution. While masculine energy has moved society forward in important ways, we have reached a point where our very survival depends upon healing the separation of, as one poet has said, "fierce brother from lost sister" (Macpherson, 35). It is difficult to make war—or to drain a heron marsh, or to redline an inner city neighborhood—when you're conjuring wind, water, and big rocks, when you feel that if you cut a tree your arm would bleed.

Should the existence of such texts, and reflection upon them, change our teaching practice? Of course; and I am certainly not the first to link feminism, nonviolence, and classroom teaching. Composition theorists have been in the forefront of this exploration. Cynthia L. Caywood and Gillian R. Overing, for example, in their anthology *Teaching Writing: Pedagogy, Gender and Equity*, have called the old fashioned model of writing-as-product "inherently authoritarian:"

> . . . certain forms of discourse and language are privileged: the expository essay is valued over the exploratory; the argumentative essay set above the autobiographical; the clear evocation of a thesis preferred to a more organic exploration of a topic; the impersonal, rational voice ranked more highly than the intimate, subjective one. The valuing of one form over another requires that the teacher be a judge, imposing a hierarchy of learned aesthetic values, gathered from ideal texts, upon the student text (xii).

Process-based pedagogies, by contrast, validate intuition and the private voice, cooperation, and full participation.

In the same anthology, even more daringly, Elisabeth Däumer and Sandra Runzo begin their essay, "Transforming the Composition Classroom" with the provocative sentence, "It is helpful to remind ourselves how much our work as teachers resembles the work of our mothers (45)." They go on to address not only the positive ramifications of that analogy—the gentle nurturing of language in an atmosphere of trust—but also its negative ones. Teaching composition relegates women yet again to the vocation of civilizer and upholder of social norms. One thinks of the drooping wife in Crane's "The Bride Comes to Yellow Sky."

Däumer and Runzo also point out how

> the description of an accomplished writing style, found in virtually any rhetorical textbook, coincides . . . with Carol Gilligan's description of what she calls the masculine mode of thought and morality. . . . Because the masculine mode of morality develops from the basic trait of separation, males learn to resolve ethical dilemmas by depersonalizing situations—by detaching themselves from others—and by trusting in an overriding structure of fair law and order. They enact a type of responsibility that is based on an assumption of aggression and adversarial relationships. The implication of Gilligan's observations is that most writing courses work toward the skillful incorporation of the masculine ethic, as Gilligan describes it, into students' writing (52–53).

Now, I'm sure all of us could cite examples that would undercut the neat categorizing of "male" and "female" moral structures delineated here. In draft counselling, for example, I have known young men to approach the decision in very personal and "connected" ways, young women to take a detached and "fair-minded" stance. And though all of us, male and female, have probably been traumatized by the blood sports of graduate school or even collegial life, though conflict and confrontation seem disturbingly central to Aristotelian debate, we might observe that classical rhetoric, like the adversarial judicial system it evolved to support, was (and remains) a way of *avoiding* physical combat. It was a better way of negotiating than Achilles and his warriors knew, and it kept the opponents at least physically intact.

In our time, though, we might well critique the classical tradition in light of nonviolent discipline. Does it silence the adversary? To silence is to sow the seeds of further tumult.

Does it humiliate? The humiliated seek revenge. Does it vanquish a minority opinion? Minorities are often right.

Since I have within me the Celtic DNA of a cruel debater, my students often have to labor with me (usually on the course evaluations) about my tendency toward rhetorical intimidation. For many of us who teach writing and literature, such a problem arises when we shift from personal writing to the modes of argument and persuasion. At this point the atmosphere of a writing group can become contaminated with heartless criticism. Here in Minnesota, students tend to become especially intransigent because they have strong Nordic inhibitions against arguing in general and against citing or demanding evidence in particular, which they conceive to be impolite. As one student laconically put it, "You don't ask a guy for his reasons. You just take his word that he has 'em."

I used to think these students were intellectually timid, and I am ashamed to say how belatedly I have come to examine the justice of their position, which essentially values, in a cold climate, the benefits of community over critical inquiry. My task now is to envision a class in argument and persuasion that supports the learner as adequately as we have learned to do in our personal essay classes. Profound, serious, and penetrating inquiry is fully compatible with gentleness, particularly if one proposes a sort of aikido model (that being the mildest of martial arts) of rhetorical contest, rather than the old-fashioned cut-and-thrust. Competition, even, is not inevitably an enemy of spirit; one of my friends, who coaches a basketball team, talks about giving "the gift of competition, which brings out the best in each player."

How to be both strong and gentle, assertive and surrendering, is a good issue to be working on; otherwise there is a danger of merely affirming the passive, the icon of woundedness. If we can work through such questions, we will be doing something useful to reunite the male and female energies that now find themselves so often bitterly divided.

I hope that my male colleagues have remained patient with me through this analysis, which I make with consciousness of the irreverence it offers the man who may be walking beside me, himself suffering the violence of men and sometimes the violence of women. As one man sadly put it, "When I was a kid the male bullies beat me up, and now when I go to conferences, the feminists beat me up." In trying to write this, I am struggling with formidable constraints of a dualistic language: male/female, fierce brother/lost sister, not to mention the burden of poor, exhausted *anima* with her Jungian baggage. More complex even than words are the slippery realities they try to pin: how can we conceptualize, much less describe, a deep ontology of gender? Without letting men off the hook, for they have a bad record in the violence department, we need to observe that the culture of war, its metaphors and modes, have determined the course of how *all* of us do business on this planet.

In repudiation of the evolving "man of feeling" who awakened somewhere around the time of Samuel Johnson, the culture of war has given us the Hemingway hero and the Marlboro Man, never snivelling, never "taken." But it's important to note that if one pays attention to the long-neglected literature written by women in wartime, there is a female version of this desensitized, desexed war robot—the Valkyrie nurse, the Amazon V.A.D. or ambulance driver. Helen Zenna Smith, in her World War I novel *Not So Quiet*, tells about the "sheltered young women who smilingly stumbled from the chintz-covered drawing-rooms straight into hell (165)." Their leader, Georgina Toshington, soon to die under fire, represents what became their ideal, a tragic twist on the civilized aspirations of the "new woman:"

> She is wandering around in the flickering candlelight dressed in a soiled woolen undervest and a voluminous pair of navy blue bloomers, chain-smoking yellow perils at a furious rate. There is something vaguely comforting in the Amazonian height and breadth of Tosh. She has the hips of a matron—intensified by

> the four pairs of thick combinations she always wears for warmth, a mind like a sewer (her own definition), the courage of a giant, the vocabulary of a Smithfield butcher, and the round, wind-reddened face of a dairymaid (11).

An American writer and V.A.D. nurse, Mary Borden, put the dislocation this way: "There are no men here, so why should I be a woman?" (60). And why are there no men? After a graphic portrayal of the mangled bodies on her ward, she concludes, "There are these things, but no men" (60).

Simone Weil's commentary on the *Iliad* was similar: "To define force—it is that x that turns anybody who is subjected to it into a *thing*" (3). The power of war to turn people into things, as she continues, is double-edged: ". . . those who use it and those who endure it are turned to stone" (25).

Men are not the problem: that x, force, is the problem. Once awakened, as by a kind of perverse witchcraft, it rips through culture with a deadly life of its own. An image rises for me from Leslie Marmon Silko's book *Ceremony*, in which the Laguna shaman attempts to "explain" the community's dislocation:

> *Finally there was only one*
> *who hadn't shown off charms or power.*
> *The witch stood in the shadows beyond the fire*
> *and no one ever knew where this witch came from*
> *which tribe*
> *or if it was a woman or a man (134).*

Silko's degendered, decultured metawitch, showing off merely, creates the ultimate nightmare: "white skin people / like the belly of a fish / covered with hair" (135). Silko's myth names the color of the earth's problem, and then its range of destruction:

> *They will carry objects*
> *which can shoot death*
> *faster than the eye can see.*

They will kill the things they fear
all the animals
the people will starve.

They will fear what they find
They will fear the people
They will kill what they fear (136).

But Silko chooses to bind the oppressed people to the source of their oppression in a symbolic chain of cause and effect. To think "that all evil resides with white people" is "the trickery of witchcraft," the shaman says. "Then we will look no farther to see what is really happening" (132).

Similarly, I think that blaming the male system will keep us from seeing what is really happening. Earlier on I said that we know more about the machine than the garden, authority than consensus, the outer than the inner, the rational than the intuitive. I suggested we explore alternative modes of operating to see what we might learn in order to get on with the gender-neutral business of saving the planet. My own explorations over the last few years have led me to live in several different versions of consensual or feminist community. Before these sojourns, I was quite idealistic about the prospect of women sitting around the tribal fire picking nits out of each other's hair. But a few weeks in feminist utopia will convince most anyone that the problem is not *men* but the self, or the self among others.

It is time for us to look carefully at what we want to protect and carry forward from the old system into a new one, as well as to anticipate the pitfalls of any brave new consensual world. Hierarchical systems tend to reward merit (which makes sense) though usually in terms of well-thumbed, "old boy" criteria (which does not). Consensual systems, conversely, sometimes represent the lowest common denominator of vision, which is not vision at all. When everyone has an equal say, discourse can fall into a sort of impoverished Esperanto. True giftedness, knowledge, and authority may be shunted aside in favor of an ideal of equality (college professors, for example, being given equal voice with auto mechanics in determining the fate of the community car). Worse yet, a consensual system can easily be held hostage by any member who chooses to impede the process. People with an axe to grind, the emotionally disturbed, even the merely verbose are much harder to manage in a circle of co-equals. Consensual decision-making requires infinite patience, integrity, and wisdom.

I'm sure many of us have met similar problems as we articulate and try to practice what I have described as nonviolent pedagogy. What then is the answer? Certainly it would be unwise to substitute an oppressive "female" system for an oppressive "male" one. But, if I have emphasized the personal, intuitive, connecting mode over the detached, rational, distancing one—and I have—if I have called one nonviolent, implying that the other is red in tooth and claw—and I have—it is because the hierarchical system is still running things. Male discourse remains the norm. As one of my friends in the legal system recently remarked, "If we went to sleep for five minutes, we'd wake up to discover that men have appointed fifty more men to the courts."

I will conclude by conceding that although hierarchical systems may not always be, of their very nature, depraved, I consider them to be on moral notice. And though consensual systems and the banal processing of insights around the feminist campfire often make me nervous and bored, I am willing to gnash my teeth a little for the sake of advancing consciousness.

If we take a long view, it seems apparent that the movement we call feminism is part of a much larger reorganizing process at work in human consciousness. The task is not to replace the male system with the female but to increase the range of humane problem solving strategies available to us all; to bring intuition into the critical process, for example, but not to exclude a rational ordering; to articulate a reasonable closure but to allow within it an element of gentle tentativeness. As all of us—women, people of color, the differently abled, differently sexed, or differently mind-mapped—find our true voices in the academic community. I think that we can expect an "eruption of spirit" (to borrow Teilhard's phrase). I have taught a few men to knit, and (I say with some chagrin) they bring to it tremendous inventiveness. Similarly, when a woman becomes an airplane mechanic, she will do the job differently because (or if) her hands are used to needlework. When you try something new, perhaps you don't know how to do it right, but, more importantly, you don't know how to do it wrong.

I look forward to an eruption of spirit, but in the short term I expect merely eruptions. Now that more voices are being heard, we have a lot of clamor. Last year women were furious at men. This year people of color are flaying white people in seminars across the academic community. Next year I cannot imagine what new chaos will arise. This does not especially bother me: I think that a truly vital organization (be it a home, a classroom, or a university) has to tolerate this kind of cacaphony, however painful in the short term. If a community is *really* multicultural and multivocal instead of just playing at it, there is going to be dissent. Women believe different things than men believe about the very nature of reality; their intellectual style is not the same. And for "women" and "men" in the preceding sentence you could substitute any racial or gender-preference opposition. When you put people of difference in a circle and ask them to talk to each other and remember, it's a recipe for pain. It was not, let me remind you, a circle of farm animals Isaiah was imaging.

I like the way Paula Gunn Allen makes this point. Being herself of Laguna, Dakota, Navajo, Lebanese, and Scots descent, her internal committee richly celebrates chaos:

> Our planet, my beloved, is in crisis; this, of course, we all know. We, many of us, think that her crisis is caused by men, or White people, or capitalism, or industrialism, or loss of spiritual vision, or social turmoil or war or psychic disease. For the most part we do not recognize that the reason for her state is that she is entering upon a great initiation—she is becoming someone else. Our

> planet, my darling, is gone coyote, *heyoka*, and it is our great honor to attend her passage rites. She is giving birth to her new consciousness of herself and her relationship to the other vast intelligences, other holy beings in her universe. Her travail is not easy, and it occasions her intensity, her conflict, her turmoil—the turmoil, conflict, and intensity that human and other creaturely life mirror . . . (54).

Heyoka. There's that word again. I am willing to risk turmoil, to go coyote, because the alternative is to die, or worse, to kill. As we try to center and recompose ourselves and our students, I think we teachers are in a race with death for the future of humankind. On the one hand, we are learning that all of us are knit together in a web of connections. We are seeing that community-building, group problem solving, and the fostering of mutual interdependence are central to our task as liberal arts teachers and vital to a positive vision of the future. At the same time, lethal forces are on the loose. We must operate under a certain urgency. I quote Gregory Bateson's essay, "Pathologies of Epistemology" in *Steps to an Ecology of Mind:*

> It is clear now to most people that there are many catastrophic dangers which have grown out of the occidental errors of epistemology. These range from insecticides to pollution, to atomic fallout, to the possibility of melting the Antarctic ice cap. . . . this massive aggregation of threats . . . arises out of errors in our habits of thought at deep and partly unconscious levels (487).

In the aftermath of the Gulf War, I am not confident (though I am hopeful) that we will win this race with death or that we can anticipate a better outcome than to stay human to the end. But a teacher of poetry awakens, with luck, a few dozen people a year from single vision and Newton's sleep. There are worse lives. When my students ask me, as they often do, to defend the usefulness of studying English, I do not reply in terms of better résumés and clearer office memos. I say, "If you learn to read texts well, there are certain con games you may not fall for . . ." "Occidental errors" Bateson more gracefully calls them. As I attempt to define one area of the moral world of literary study, I hope to affirm the usefulness of a profession dedicated to exploring habits of thought at deep and partly unconscious levels. This preoccupation has a social context and a crucial function. In a lethal world, as M. C. Richards has said, poetry is necessary to survival.

I had a dream. I don't know if it was a dream about the end of things or the beginning. For a while I thought the dream was about nuclear holocaust, but, then again, maybe it was just a routine dream about teaching. In the dream I seemed to be living in a cave. I was no longer young, but there was a baby, hanging on to my long grey braid, and a boy of about twelve years old. At night we looked for animal eyes in the darkness outside the circle of firelight at the cave mouth. Then, in the morning we got up and went outside. The boy and I sat down and we began to scratch in the dirt with a stick.

Through my dreamer's eyes, I peer to see what I have written in the dirt. *It is the alphabet, in Greek.*

We are always starting over.

Epilogue

The Booty of the Dove

Home is the riddle of the wise—the booty of the dove.
—Emily Dickinson (717)

From one margin of the world to the other, Black Hole School to a shelter for the city's street people, most of whom are probably my "emotionally disturbed" students grown up . . .

I have come to St. Francis Center—a "living room," as they call it, for the homeless, chronically alcoholic, and mentally ill—to teach writing. I came at first with the idealistic fantasy that there would be a lot of creativity on the street. I came because I believe that finding voice as a writer means gaining a small space of freedom and self-determination. I wanted to give sanity away instead of a tax-deductible contribution and tins of pumpkin pie filling. The usual delusion.

I have come because I've seen sometimes, back in my university world, the edge of a frightening abyss: surveying, for example, the work students bring back from oral history projects. They've interviewed elderly people about the significant events of their lives, and "How did you feel about that?" my students, good consumers of the morning TV talk shows, have asked the old people. How did you feel about the war, the Depression, the concentration camp, the first child? "I felt NOTHING," certain people will say. "I don't remember that I thought about it at all."

Some of the respondents may of course be bashful or merely unwilling to talk to earnest students, but I think that something more sad and dangerous is often happening at the edge of Nothing. For many in the generation before ours, there existed no instrument for inner articulation. And thus there could be, for many, no inner world in the sense a contemporary person would perceive that inscape—or that a medieval person, for that matter, with quill in hand or merely space to speak and be heard in, would perceive it. Lacking the space, the pen, the listener, our spirits atrophy. These old people who remember "nothing"—are they dried up and longing for death? Have they lived at all? What have they done to their own children? I ask because I know that in order to learn to listen we must first be *listened to.* When I work with prisoners and other deeply damaged people, I often sense they do not value their inner worlds or that they do not have them: who can tell which? "Nothing," they say to me. I have called this "nothing" *dangerous* because I know that such silenced people cannot respect the inner world of others, individuality, consciousness, or the person. Silenced, no doubt, by every species of violence, they harm others in their turn.

It's often impossible to teach writing to people living under such constraints or to give them poems. Quickly we cut to the fingerpainting. Almost everyone has inner images, and from these images a story can be led out, perhap a vision that pleases, that brings a smile. There must be a mirror to show the soul to itself before the soul can begin to gather its courage.

This is not about "helping." Ivan Illich once told a bunch of us starry-eyed college students, "Don't even dream of helping. You have nothing to give. Dream of learning."

Let me share, then, a little of the flavor of yet another school where I am blundering through a study of this matter:

January

Most of my students at St. Francis Center have turned out to be docile and imitative writers. Their work rings predictable changes on plots that spill from TV, for TV runs incessantly in every shelter, hospital, asylum, and rehab center. These writers are obsessed, moreover, with correctness; they complain when the pencils I bring in don't have erasers.

I meet with them in a circle because I believe that a writing group—the kind we work with nowadays in high school and college and professional life—can be a challenging and cherishing community. But I have never before sat in a writing group where the students carry weapons. "Docile," I have called Steve, Lucas, and Mark: "Ma'am," they say, and open doors for me. But Mark is dour and growls when any writing buddy sits too close. Lucas is fresh from prison (he proudly tells me), and yesterday's knife fight at St. Francis Center was over a stolen bingo card.

This day I have brought a writing project I developed, during a stint of grade school teaching, from the work of Sylvia Ashton-Warner. Ashton-Warner, a New Zealander, taught Maori children to read by finding out what words they needed to control. She made a primer out of the words that linked them to fear or ecstasy, witchcraft or the passions of love.

My version of this exercise asks students to write down on small slips of paper the words they like. Then they paste their words on a piece of construction paper, adding connectives or drawings as they like. For inspiration I have brought some poems that combine words and images. The exercise is easy to do with young children, but it is sophisticated enough for serious writers.

But where is my class today? Mark and Lucas are in detox; Steve is playing chess with himself in the corner. "You can tell the guys who've been in jail," Lucas has told me, "because they all play chess."

"Andy? Do you want to work with me? Write, or draw?" Andy is about twenty. He wears filthy dreadlocks and his skin is covered with a grey veil of dirt. He winces if you talk to him. As always, he slides away from my question, then slips in a counter question: "What kind of writing?" But when I look he is gone, like the angels that appear from time to time in one's peripheral vision.

In the end I have only one taker, a man named Paul sitting in the corner of the room, who responds to my invitation as though I had offered him a present. "Oh, YES, thank you. I'd like to very much." Paul is slight, about thirty-five, and has matted hair that sticks out on his forehead like the bill of a cap. His polyester shirt is too small for him, and the buttons strain across his chest. What's most disconcerting is his right eye, unfocused and buried in swollen tissue. It oozes pus, which he keeps trying to wipe away.

Paul writes the following words: *one, two, stop, go, digitalis, Paulie, now, hart, faiful.* I sit and work beside him. From my own hoard of words, he borrows *prairie.*

As he works, Paul tells me about his life as an engineer on the man-made island of Britannia near the tip of Japan. He tells of his battles with the head-hunters and cannibals there. Worse, he tells me that the head-hunters are now invading the Minneapolis suburbs, arriving in business suits, with concealed blowguns. He is always having to go and fight them hand-to-hand. You can tell a head-hunter, no matter how cleverly disguised, by making him spit on a tissue. If it disappears—the spit? the tissue? I hesitate to ask—that's the *sign.*

By now he is drawing elaborate crystalline structures in many colors on his construction paper, prisoning or enshrining the words inside. I don't usually ask people about their words when I do this exercise, afraid of getting too nosy and psychological. But I want to know about the word *faiful,* which, upside down, I read as *falafel.* Has Paul been hanging out behind a Lebanese deli?

"*Faiful,*" Paul reads obediently, like a good child asked to spell a word and use it in a sentence. "I would like to have a *faiful* friend."

When we are done, he hangs his words and his crystals on the St. Francis Center bulletin board.

"What's your favorite word, Paul?"

"NOW," he says. "Now now now."

Clara, the social worker from Client Services, takes me aside to check up on Paul. "He seldom talks to anyone. How is he doing?"

"He's OK," I say, noncommitally. Sitting daily in this living room, I have picked up the evasive shrug and loyalties that shut out cop and social worker. "Maybe we should get a doctor to look at his eye." I don't really want to talk to her about Paul's words or his business. That's as "faiful" as I can be.

"We're trying to get him committed," Clara says apologetically. Involuntary commitment is an embarrassing subject at St. Francis Center. "Just to get him *started.* Most of the time we can't get him to sleep inside, even. He sleeps in the Selby tunnel."

When I walk to my bus stop in stinging snow, I will pass the tunnel mouth, unlighted, seemingly abandoned, but full of eyes.

February

There is no question of teaching writing any more. There are not enough erasers in the world. So we paint and color—very popular activities—talk, play bingo.

"Why do you come here?" one of the guys asks me. He is a Hispanic man who draws intricate and beautiful scenes of palm trees and parrots, which he always tears up at the end of the day.

"Juan, I don't know. It's a good way to be with people." I'm ashamed of all the reasons that brought me at first: to teach, to understand, to spy, to feel better. Now I come out of dumb instinct, with what the Zen masters call "beginner's mind." And friendship. I like Juan, and Paul, and Lucas, and Andy, who is a year or so older than my son: my life is linked with theirs in some obscure way. For the record, I don't like murderous Mark, and I'm relatively indifferent to Clara, the social worker. I'm devoted to Stew, a Mennonite volunteer, and to Seth, probably the nuttiest human being in the city, who spends his days cutting newspaper into tiny elfish paperdolls, who dresses in shreds of motley, and who has the air of someone famous in disguise. Why do I come here? This has become my community, my un-writing group. "Juan, I don't know."

I'm a single parent, alone a lot. I don't like parties; they make me feel unreal. I like being with people, though, and I like making art out of old candy wrappers and trash. "Are you lonely?" Juan pursues.

Since I'm afraid he'll ask me for a date, I dodge that one. "Not at the moment." By temperament, fate, or possibly vocation, I'm a solitary. But I don't feel like explaining all that to Juan.

March

Today, I sit for a long time talking to Becky. I don't usually just sit with people. I'd rather keep my hands busy with the finger paints. But Becky has lured me with the bait of wanting help with a job application, and so we begin to talk about her life.

The conversation is giving me flashbacks. When I was ten or twelve there was a school field—once prairie—near my house where a kildeer nested. If my sister and I approached the nest, the kildeer would pretend to have a broken wing and stagger along the ground, trying to lure us away from her eggs.

People seem to do the same dance. I guess I do it myself, and maybe that's why I get mad when someone drags me into it down at St. Francis Center, where the Kildeer Dance often headlines the floor show. Not wanting to confess the real pain, we wallow in phony pain. (It's *we* now. I've gone over, like Damian, to the side of the so-called lepers.)

"I think I'm pregnant," Becky confides. "I hope I am; it would give me something to pass my days."

She has been sitting for an hour, slack-jawed, staring. Her face is small and attractive, though vacuous, her hair peroxided to bronze with a few inches of dark root. Looking at her body crumpled in the chair, I can't tell if she is pregnant, heavy, or simply sliding back to earth the way some women seem to do. She smells stale and greasy. So do I, of course, by now.

"I miscarried three times. I had a baby who lived only three days . . ."

Why do I think this is not true? A kildeer crying nowhere near the nest?

". . . I took a beating. I took twelve blows to my head with a baseball bat. I've had plastic surgery all over my face."

Does she catch me searching her face for scars?

"I've got bumps on my head. You could feel them. I can feel them, anyhow. The baby's legs were broken, her back was broken. She only lived a few days."

"Are you getting some prenatal care?" I ask.

"I don't want to bother with WIC. It's too much hassle."

"The man you're with, is he OK about the baby?"

She begins a confusing story. "I was afraid to tell him. He thinks I was sleeping with this other guy. I did sleep in the guy's bed, but we had a board between us"—like Tristan and Isolde, it occurs to me—"He's so fat. He's three times as big as me. He makes my skin crawl."

"But the man you're with?"

"Oh, he wants the baby very badly. He makes me eat calves' liver."

"Better you than me."

"I hope I'm pregnant. It will give me something to pass my days."

She tells me about the temporary work she does, making

sandwiches for a take-out lunch place. Becky is the sort of person the welfare reformers might point a finger at. She *could* hold down a full-time job, they would say.

But could she? Would she make friends at work? Who would listen to her monologues, her kildeer cry? As we talk through the job application, I see her in my mind's eye at the luncheonette, with plastic gloves on her hands, packing sandwiches, the other women avoiding her as the kids must have avoided her on the playground. I see her going home to bundle with her fat man.

There is a new young worker in Client Services. He is worried about Becky. "Did you get your food? Do you need more?"

"No, she's pregnant, though," I tell him. "She needs nice vegetables."

"How am I going to get this food home?" Becky whines when the new young worker hands her the bag. I know that in a few minutes she will have gotten him to drive her. He's given her a lot of nice frozen shrimp and the best canned goods.

"Can you come around the back?" I hear him say. "I'll pick you up in my car."

Later in March

I go to a conference on college writing in Boston to see if I can learn more about teaching Seth and Andy and Becky, as well as the university students on my day job. For this annual migration, English teachers from all over the country board planes at the exorbitant rates geared for business travel. We stay at hotels designed along the lines of theme parks; we ride up and down in glass elevators strung with holiday lights. The hotels are attached to shopping malls and movie theaters so that we can catch up on what's in and what's out and buy things. "Are they still showing glitter on the legs?" I hear an elegantly dressed woman ask a salesperson at Neiman Marcus, and I wonder, Who are *they*? That's a theme assignment I sometimes give in English 101—Tell me, who are *they*?—so I am always looking for data.

What they're showing at the conference this year is the idea that identity is merely a social consensus, that there is no stable ego, that we are defined by our social roles, that Socrates, praying for the inner and outer man to be at peace, was apparently off track. I hear this kind of thing at session after session. Indeed, as I ride up and down on the elevators meeting images of myself in the shiny mirrors that cover every plane surface, my sense of a stable identity begins to slide. I think, for starters, that I really have to put on some decent stockings, which brings me to the lingerie counter at Neiman Marcus. Everything costs more than at home on the prairie, and nothing comes in a familiar white plastic egg, so I quickly buy the cheapest stockings I see. In the restroom I discover that they are the kind you have to have a garter belt for. What to do? I knot them above the knees as I have seen old ladies do.

I go to hear a paper on the personal essay, which attempts to convince me that Orwell never really shot that elephant and that I have no right to expect Truth in the personal essay: to do so is "puritanical." (Will this concept help me to deconstruct Becky's discourse?) I start to daydream about a sermon I read once by an eighteenth-century Puritan preacher. It was about the evils of stained glass church windows and how they change the holy light. (How much would it matter to you if I were making this all up?)

"Liberatory pedagogy" is also out, I hear. That was last year's fad: encouraging students to sit in a circle and talk about their own experience as a bridge to the academic texts. Our students are wealthier than we are, one young man alleges in his paper, so what do they have to be liberated from? I can tell you the answer to that because I wrote it down in my notebook once. This is Colman McCarthy's commentary on Paulo Freire: "Little oppression is found here in comparison with the severity of northeast Brazil, but we share a common culture of silence. Wealth, not poverty, is making objects out of most of us: who can keep count of, let alone actively resist, all the outrages?" (148). As I flop on a sofa near the women's restroom, I overhear a famous scholar define his agenda to a group of admirers: "It's time to get rid of these marginal students. If they can't learn academic writing, the hell with them. The next round of budget cuts should give us our chance."

The Desert Fathers used to say when confronted with an uncongenial discourse community, "Flee, be silent. . . ." For my part, I flee each night to a small student hostel in Beacon Hill, a twenty-minute walk from the conference. The student hostel is not silent; it is full of subdued rock music and graduate students discussing phenomenology. I make friends with Paul and Aziz, and we sit up half the night talking about the ideas of Bernard Lonergan. The next day I sneak Paul into the conference to hear a debate about academic discourse. Paul is trying to encourage his colleagues in philosophy to be more plain and clear, to speak from experience rather than from abstract generalization. Back among the English teachers, though, we sense a growing mistrust of allowing personal experience into the classroom. "Sentimental realism," someone sneers.

Paul and I walk back to the hostel. It's very cold, sleeting, in Boston. An old man sitting on the sidewalk grabs my coat and asks for change. We go into the coffee shop and buy a cup of the fancy roast they sell and take it out and wrap his fingers around it. We talk awhile and he grabs my hand. I feel no fear, but I feel a metaphysical resistance: I do not want to be pulled in.

April

We are talking about Wordsworth in my class at the university. I have asked students to write about any childhood experiences that connect them to the "Ode: Intimations of Immortality." One bright, spectacled, male, pre-law student writes, in general but provocative terms, about losing his sense of self as he goes through school: "The raw feelings get a callus. . . ." A Southeast Asian female student, who has just turned in a near-perfect exam on Descartes (though she has trouble writing academic discourse) writes about being bound and gagged by her parents to keep her from crying when the family escaped from Vietnam. As she lay under her brothers and sisters on the boat, something sour kept dripping on her face. "Vomit," she prints carefully in parentheses.

In my class at St. Francis Center, somebody has started a fad for opening wallets, showing off pictures of lost children, Christmas trees, proms, anniversaries, and other artifacts of sentimental realism: the booty of the dove. Seth is cutting out his intricate paperdolls. The living room is pretty quiet.

A few months ago as I rode the bus downtown to join the annual *Messiah* sing-along, Seth got on. My first impulse was to spring up and greet him; my second was to bury my face in the Handel score. I was riding with my friend Kathy, a county judge. Would she think I was crazy? Would Seth? Would I be showing off my friendship with a street person? Would Seth deny me? By the time I processed all these subtle questions, Seth had gotten off the bus.

Today, with spring coming on, Becky has found shelter in a Catholic Worker community. Lucas is dead, crushed by a garbage truck. Andy, with the dreadlocks, is also missing. One frigid winter night, all the shelter directors had gotten on the phone to each other and agreed to shut Andy out on the street. That way, the police would be obliged to put him in the hospital. It's a quick way to engineer an involuntary commitment. I had seen it in the paper with a photo of the police patting him down for weapons. My son adjusted his glasses and peered into the mystery of the news; he, too, works at the Center: "Is that *our* Andy? He hates to be touched."

He is our Andy, and I suspect that we are his. The man who grabbed my hand in Boston, too, has hold of me. We are time-warped together, partners in a dance.

Today my young daughter has come to paint with us. She

collaborates for a while with Seth on paper dolls. "I like him, but you won't bring him home, will you?" she asks behind her hand.

I pretend not to hear, not to know. I didn't even have the courage to talk to Seth on the bus. Cozy in the St. Francis living room, we watch the people passing on the street, looking in, looking away.

"Why do you come here?" one of the Native American women asks me.

"Marie, I don't know. It's a good place to be with people."

One or Two Things

1

Don't bother me
I've just
been born.

2

The butterfly's loping flight
carries it through the country of the leaves
delicately, and well enough to get it
where it wants to go, wherever that is, stopping
here and there to fuzzle the damp throats
of flowers and the black mud; up
and down it swings, frenzied and aimless; and sometimes

for long delicious moments it is perfectly
lazy, riding motionless in the breeze on the soft stalk
of some ordinary flower.

3

The god of dirt
came up to me many times and said
so many wise and delectable things, I lay
on the grass listening
to his dog voice,
crow voice,
frog voice; *now*,
he said, and *now*,
and never once mentioned *forever*,

4

which has nevertheless always been
like a sharp iron hoof,
at the center of my mind.

5

One or two things are all you need
to travel over the blue pond, over the deep

roughage of the trees and through the stiff
flowers of lightning—some deep
memory of pleasure, some cutting
knowledge of pain.

6

But to lift the hoof!
For that you need an idea.

7

For years and years I struggled
just to love my life. And then

the butterfly
rose, weightless, in the wind.
"Don't love your life
too much," it said,

and vanished
into the world.

—Mary Oliver (50–51)

Works Cited

Auden, W. H. *Academic Graffiti.* New York: Random House, 1972.

———. *Collected Poems.* Edited by Edward Mendelson. New York: Random House, 1976.

Augustine of Hippo. *The Confessions of St. Augustine.* Translated by Rex Warner. New York: Mentor-NAL-Penguin, 1963.

Allen, Paula Gunn. "The Woman I Love is a Planet; The Planet I Love is a Tree." In *Reweaving the World: The Emergence of Ecofeminism.* Edited by Irene Diamond and Gloria Feman Orenstein. San Francisco: Sierra, 1990.

Allen, Woody. "Americana." *Time Magazine* 113:25. (February 26, 1979), 25.

Bachelard, Gaston. *"L'air et les songes." On Poetic Imagination and Reverie.* Translated by Colette Gaudin. New York: Bobbs-Merrill, 1971.

Bateson, Gregory. *Steps to an Ecology of Mind.* New York: Ballantine, 1972.

Belenky, Mary Field, et. al. *Women's Ways of Knowing: The Development of Self, Voice and Mind.* New York: Basic, 1986.

Bernheimer, Martin. "Fonteyn Was an Artist of Supreme Refinement." *Minneapolis Tribune*, 3 March 1991, 1–2F.

Borden, Mary. *The Forbidden Zone.* London: Heinemann, 1929.

Brown, Joseph Epes. *The Spiritual Legacy of the American Indian.* Wallingford, PA: Pendle Hill, 1964.

Brueggemann, Walter. *The Prophetic Imagination.* Philadelphia: Fortress Press, 1981.

Caywood, Cynthia, and Gillian R. Overing, eds. *Teaching Writing: Pedagogy, Gender and Equity.* New York: SUNY, 1987.

Crane, Stephen. *The Red Badge of Courage: An Episode of the American Civil War.* 2nd ed. New York: Norton, 1982.

Davies, Robertson. *The Salterton Trilogy.* New York: Viking Penguin, 1987.

Dickinson, Emily. *The Letters of Emily Dickinson.* Vol. 3. Edited by Thomas H. Johnson. Cambridge: Harvard (Belknap), 1958.

Dillard, Annie. *The Writing Life.* New York: Harper & Row, 1989.

Dunne, Tad. *Lonergan and Spirituality: Towards a Spiritual Integration.* Chicago: Loyola, 1985.

Elbow, Peter. "The Pleasures of Voice in the Literary Essay." In *Literary Nonfiction: Theory, Criticism, Pedagogy.* Edited by Chris Anderson. Carbondale: Southern Illinois U., 1989.

Eliot, T. S. *Collected Poems 1909–1962.* New York: Harcourt, 1963.

———. *Selected Essays.* New York: Harcourt, 1964.

Euripedes. *The Bacchae.* Translated by Michael Cacoyannis. New York: NAL, 1982.

Evely, Louis. *In His Presence.* Translated by J. F. Stevenson. New York: Herder and Herder, 1970.

Farber, Jerry. *The Student as Nigger.* New York: Pocket Books, 1970.

Forché, Carolyn. "The Colonel." *The Country Between Us.* New York: Harper, 1981.

Forster, E. M. *Howards End.* New York: Vintage–Knopf/Random House, 1921.

Freiere, Paulo. *Pedagogy of the Oppressed.* New York: Herder, 1972.

Fussell, Paul. *The Great War and Modern Memory.* New York: Oxford, 1975.

Gilligan, Carol. *In a Different Voice: Psychological Theory and Women's Development.* Cambridge: Harvard, 1982.

Goddard, Harold L. "A Pre-Freudian Reading of 'The Turn of the Screw.'" In Henry James *The Turn of the Screw.* Edited by Richard Kimbrough. New York: Norton, 1966.

Goethe, Johann Wolfgang Von. *Faust.* In *The Ascent of Man: Sources and Interpretations.* Edited by John F. Hanrahan, New York: Little, Brown, 1975.

Goldberg, Natalie. *Writing Down the Bones.* Boston: Shambhala, 1986.

Hall, Arnold. "Training for Non Violence." In *The Pursuit of Peace: A Book of Current Knowledge and Interests for Group Study.* London: Drayton House, 1975.

Hall, Nor. *The Moon and the Virgin: Reflections on the Archetypal Feminine.* New York: Harper and Row, 1980.

Havel, Václav. "The End of the Modern Era." *New York Times,* 1 March 1992, E15.

Hopkins, Gerard Manley. *The Poems of Gerard Manley Hopkins.* Edited by W. H. Gardner and N. H. MacKenzie. 4th ed. New York: Oxford, 1956.

Hemingway, Ernest. *A Farewell to Arms.* New York: Scribners, 1969.

Hyde, Lewis. *The Gift: Imagination and the Erotic Life of Property.* 5th ed. New York: Vintage–Random House, 1983.

Kelly, Thomas. *A Testament of Devotion.* New York: Harper, 1941.

Kinnell, Galway. "St. Francis and the Sow." In *Mortal Acts, Mortal Words.* Boston: Houghton Mifflin, 1980.

Lao-Tzu. *Tao Te Ching.* Translated by Isabella Mears. Wheaton, IL: Theosophical Publishing House, 1971.

Larkin, Philip. *The Whitsun Weddings.* London: Faber, 1964.

Lawrence, Barbara. "Four Letter Words Can Hurt You." In *Current Issues and Enduring Questions: Methods and Models of Argument.* Edited by Sylvan Barnet and Hugo Bedau. 2nd ed. Boston: Bedford–St. Martin's, 1990.

MacNeice, Louis. *Collected Poems 1925–1948.* London: Faber and Faber, 1949.

Macpherson, Jay. *The Boatman.* Oxford: Canada, NDG. In Laurence Perrine. *Sound and Sense: An Introduction to Poetry.* 6th ed. New York: Harcourt, 1982.

Macrorie, Ken. *Telling Writing.* 3rd ed. Rochelle Park, N.J.: Hayden, 1976.

Marcus, Jane. "Corpus/Corps/Corpse: Writing the Body in/at War." Afterward to *Not So Quiet . . . Stepdaughters of War*, by Helen Zenna Smith. New York: Feminist Press–CUNY, 1989.

Marx, Karl. *The Communist Manifesto.* Translated by Samuel Moore. Washington: Regnery Gateway, 1987.

Mather, Eleanore Price. *Pendle Hill: A Quaker Experiment in Community*. Wallingford, PA: Pendle Hill, 1980.

McCarthy, Colman. *Inner Companions.* Washington, D.C.: Acropolis, 1975.

Miller, Alice. *For Your Own Good: Hidden Cruelty in Child-Rearing and the Roots of Violence.* Translated by Hildegarde and Hunter Hannum. 2nd ed. New York: Farrar, Straus, Giroux, 1985.

Nh'ât Hanh, Thich. *Being Peace.* Berkeley: Parallax, 1987.

———. *The Miracle of Mindfulness.* Boston: Beacon, 1976.

Oliver, Mary. *Dream Work.* New York: Atlantic Monthly, 1986.

Ottinger, Henry. "In Short, Why Did the Class Fail?" *New York Times*, 22 July 1971, L33.

Owen, Wilfred. *The Collected Poems of Wilfred Owen.* New York: New Directions, 1965.

Palmer, Parker J. "Meeting for Learning: Education in a Quaker Context." *The Pendle Hill Bulletin* 284 (May, 1976): 1–7.

Penington, Isaac. *Works.* 4 vols. In *Quaker Spirituality*. Edited by Douglas V. Steere. New York: Paulist, 1984.

Perry, William G., Jr. "Examsmanship and the Liberal Arts," in *The Norton Reader.* 4th ed. Edited by Arthur M. Eastman. New York: Norton, 1977.

Richards, Mary Caroline. Quoted by Paulus Berenson, lecturing at Pendle Hill, November 13, 1987.

Robinson, Edward. *The Original Vision: A Study of the Religious Experience of Childhood.* Oxford, England: Manchester College, 1977.

Roethke, Theodore. *The Collected Poems of Theodore Roethke.* New York: Doubleday, 1966.

Sertillanges, A. G. *The Intellectual Life: Its Spirit, Conditions, Methods*. 5th ed. Translated by Mary Ryan. Westminster, Md.: Christian Classics, 1980.

Shaughnessy, Mina P. *Errors and Expectations: A Guide for the Teacher of Basic Writing*. New York: Oxford, 1977.

Silko, Leslie Marmon. *Ceremony*. New York: Penguin, 1986.

Soelle, Dorothee. *The Strength of the Weak: Toward a Christian Feminist Identity*. Translated by Robert and Rita Kimber. Philadelphia: Westminster, 1984.

Sophocles. *Antigone*. Translated by Elizabeth Wyckoff. New York: Simon and Schuster (Pocket Books), 1970.

Smith, Helen Zenna [Evadne Price]. *Not So Quiet . . . Stepdaughters of War.* New York: Feminist Press-CUNY, 1989.

Thomas, Dylan. *The Poems of Dylan Thomas*. 4th ed. New York: Dutton, 1966.

Tolstoy, Leo. "The Three Questions." In *Twenty-three Tales*. New York: Oxford, 1975.

Walker, Alice. *The Color Purple*. New York: Simon and Schuster, 1982.

Weil, Simone. *The Iliad or The Poem of Force*. Wallingford, PA: Pendle Hill, 1983.

———. "Spiritual Autobiography." In *The Simone Weil Reader.* Edited by George A. Panichas. New York: David McKay, 1977.

Whitman, Walt. *Complete Poetry and Collected Prose*. Edited by Justin Kaplan. New York: Library of America, 1982.

Williams, William Carlos. "Spring and All." In *Imaginations*. New York: New Directions, 1970.

Woolf, Virginia. "Thoughts of Peace in an Air Raid." In *The Death of the Moth and Other Essays*. New York: Harcourt, 1970.

———. *A Room of One's Own*. New York: Harvest/HBJ, 1989.

Woolman, John. *The Journal of John Woolman and a Plea for the Poor.* Secaucus, N.J.: Citadel, 1901.

———. "The Journal of John Woolman." In *Quaker Spirituality*. Edited by Douglas Steere. New York: Paulist, 1984.

Yeats, W. B. *The Collected Poems*. New York: Macmillan, 1956.

Woolman, John. *The Journal of John Woolman and a Plea for the Poor.* Secaucus, N.J.: Citadel, 1901.

———. "The Journal of John Woolman." In *Quaker Spirituality*. Edited by Douglas Steere. New York: Paulist, 1984.

Yeats, W. B. *The Collected Poems.* New York: Macmillan, 1956.

Credits

"This is Not Your Father's War" by Mary Rose O'Reilley first appeared in slightly different form in *Friends Journal* 37(5):7–8, 1991. Reprinted by permission of the author and *Friends Journal*, Philadelphia, PA.

"The Booty of the Dove" by Mary Rose O'Reilley. From *Weavings: A Journal of the Christian Spiritual Life* VI(6):14–20, 1991. Reprinted by permission of the author and The Upper Room, Nashville, TN.

"For Wounded Veteran, War Never Died" by Mary Rose O'Reilley appeared in a slightly different form in the *Star Tribune* (17 February 1991). Reprinted by permission of the *Star Tribune*, Minneapolis, MN.

Page 10: Excerpts from "Prayer Before Birth" by Louis MacNeice in *Collected Poems of Louis MacNeice*, edited by E. R. Dodds. Published by Faber and Faber Ltd. Reprinted by permission.

Pages 34 and 183: "Dulce et Decorum Est." *Wilfred Owen: Collected Poems of Wilfred Owen*. Copyright © 1963 by Chatto and Windus, Ltd. Reprinted by permission of New Directions Publishing Corporation.

Page 118: "The Force that Through the Green Fuse Drives the Flower." *Dylan Thomas: Poems of Dylan Thomas*. Copyright © 1945 by the Trustees for the Copyrights of Dylan Thomas. Reprinted by permission of New Directions Publishing Corporation.

Page 119: "God's Grandeur." From *The Poems of Gerard Manley Hopkins*. Copyright © 1956. Published by Oxford University Press.

Page 121: "The Shield of Achilles" by W. H. Auden. From *Collected Poems* by W. H. Auden. Copyright © 1952 by W. H. Auden. Reprinted by permission of Random House, Inc.

Page 123: "A Poem in October." *Dylan Thomas: Poems of Dylan Thomas*. Copyright © 1945 by the Trustees for the Copyrights of Dylan Thomas. Reprinted by permission of New Directions Publishing Corporation.

Page 133: "A Dialogue of Self and Soul" reprinted with permission of Macmillan Publishing Company from *The Poems of W. B. Yeats: A New Edition*, edited by Richard J. Finneran. Copyright © 1933 by Macmillan Publishing Company, renewed 1961 by Bertha Georgia Yeats.

Page 141: "The Colonel" from *The Country Between Us* by Carolyn Forche. Copyright © 1980 by Carolyn Forche. Reprinted by permission of HarperCollins Publishers.

Page 153: Excerpt from "St. Francis and the Sow," *Mortal Acts, Mortal Words* by Galway Kinnell. Copyright © 1980 by Galway Kinnell. Reprinted by permission of Houghton Mifflin Co. All rights reserved.

Page 172: "Academic Graffiti: by W. H. Auden. From *Collected Poems* by W. H. Auden. Copyright © 1960 by W. H. Auden. Reprinted by permission of Random House, Inc.

Page 180: Excerpt from "MCMXIV" in *The Whitsun Weddings* by Philip Larkin. Published by Faber & Faber Ltd. Reprinted by permission.

Page 181: "Mental Cases." From *Wilfred Owen: Collected Poems of Wilfred Owen*. Copyright © 1963 by Chatto and Windus, Ltd. Reprinted by permission of New Directions Publishing Corporation.

Also available from Boynton/Cook. . .

An Unquiet Pedagogy
Transforming Practice in the English Classroom
Eleanor Kutz & Hephzibah Roskelly
Foreword by **Paulo Freire**

An Unquiet Pedagogy argues for a new approach to teaching English in the high school and college classroom, one that reconceives the relationship of literacy and the learner. The title is taken from an essay by Paulo Freire in his book with Donald Macedo entitled *Literacy: Reading the Word and the World.* Like Freire, the authors believe that pedagogy must be critical—that it must examine the assumptions that teachers and students bring to any educational enterprise, that it must take into account the contexts of learners' lives, and that it must question, rather than quietly accept, existing practices.

Voices of beginning and experienced teachers are heard often in the book, exploring how such an unquiet pedagogy might come to be. The authors examine the experiences of these teachers, as well as their own, showing how the classroom can become a place of inquiry for both teachers and students, and how theory and research that provide an integrated perspective on language, literacy, and culture must inform teaching practice. Their aim is to transform the English classroom into a place where the imagination becomes central, and where learners construct knowledge in the development of real literacy.

0-86709-277-7 1991 Paper

The Violence of Literacy
J. Elspeth Stuckey

This book counters most of our prevailing views about literacy. It says that literacy, rather than enfranchising people, is violent, ulterior, and uniquely devoted to Western economic ends. It claims that the literacy profession perpetuates injustice, whether it knows it or not.

This is a book for anyone who thinks that reading and writing are important to learning. In this respect, it's a book for everyone, but it's primarily for people on the hotseat—English teachers, especially composition/writing/rhetoric teachers, and teachers of dropouts, adults and minorities. The book addresses economics and social class, the political structure in which English teaching fits, the character of labor, the psychology or psychotherapy of literacy, and the future of social freedom in America.

This is an angry book written by an angry English teacher: The author is angry that literacy is the center of the storm; angry that the center of the storm foments nothing but itself; angry that most of what we do, even the good that we do, remains academic, powerless, and self-serving.

What solutions are offered? The author argues that literacy is not the solution. She argues that economics is the agenda, that the ability to read and write is less important than the ability to pay. The reality is that those who set the agenda use literacy and literacy standards to maintain privilege and parcel disadvantage. The violence of literacy becomes, therefore, the customary domain of those who foresee no real change while foretelling it.

0-86709-270-X 1991 Paper

Heinemann-Boynton/Cook
361 Hanover Street
Portsmouth, NH 03801-3912

(800) 541-2086

■ ■